# Mandala Happiness 1

## Mandala Coloring Book

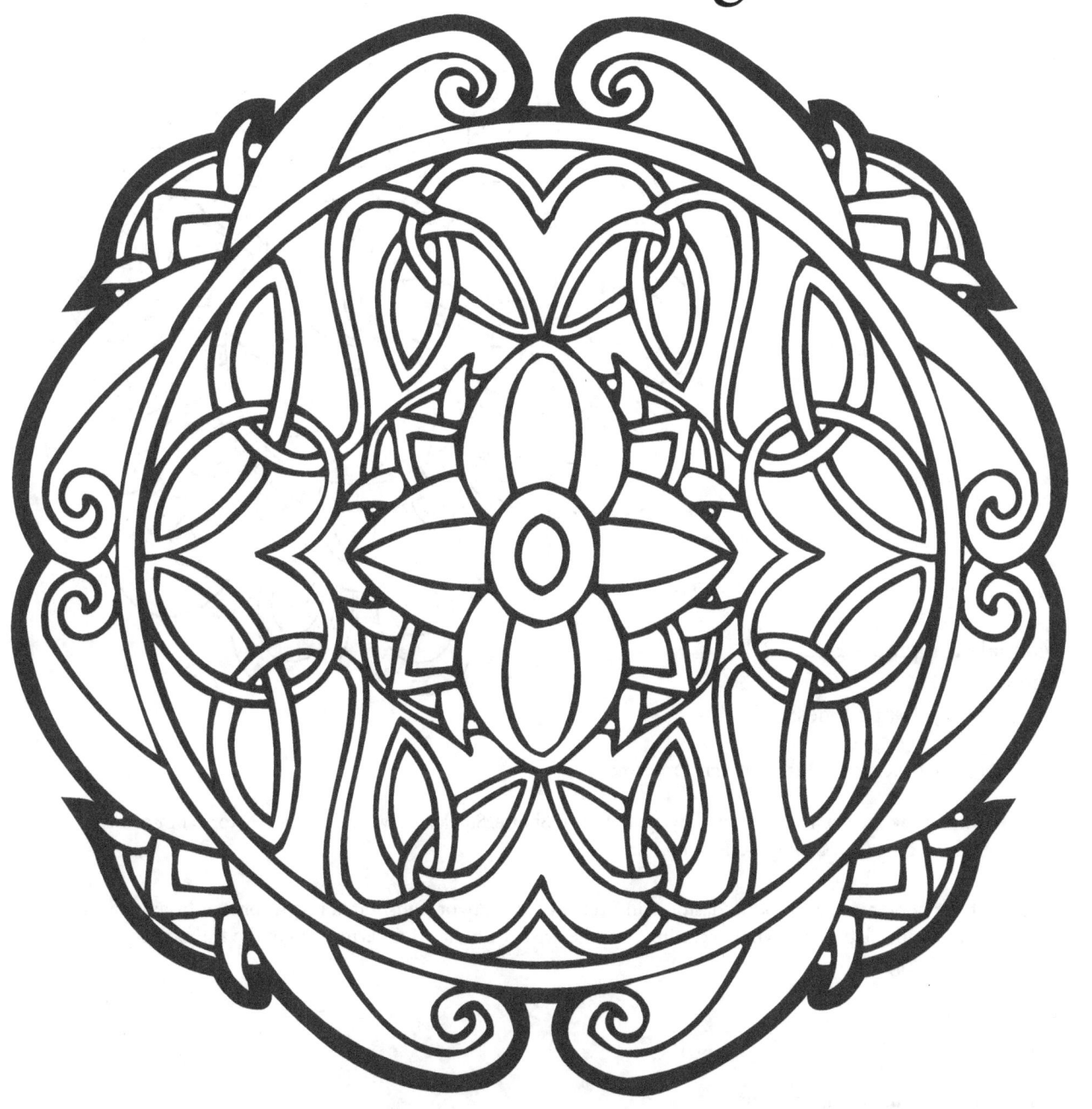

Created by J. Bruce Jones

MandalaHappiness.com

Dear Reader,

Thank you for buying Mandala Happiness 1. I hope you have fun coloring the mandalas.

I enjoy receiving comments and suggestions from readers. Your ideas are always very helpful. I also love to hear how you are using our books. Are you coloring just for fun or using it to help reduce stress, be inspired or get in touch with your artistic side?

So let me know - the good and the bad - and I will try to make even better books!

Thank you and keep coloring.

Bruce
bruce@bjdesign.com

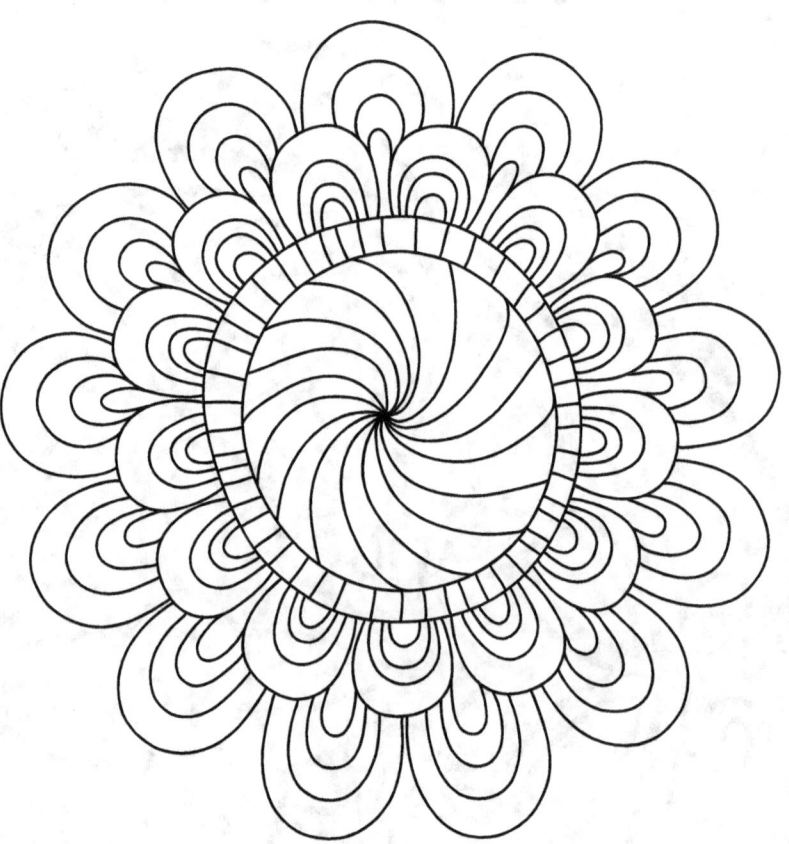

Mandala Happiness 1
Volume 1
Created By J. Bruce Jones

Images in this book are from and under copyright of www.ShutterStock and www.GraphicsFactory.com
© ShutterStock.com 2015, © GraphicsFactory.com 2015

Bruce Jones Design
661 Washington Street
Norwood, MA 02062
781-255-7171 • bruce@bjdesign.com

Check out all our cool mandala books at www.MandalaHappiness.com

# Sample Mandalas from Mandala Happiness 1
## Volume 1

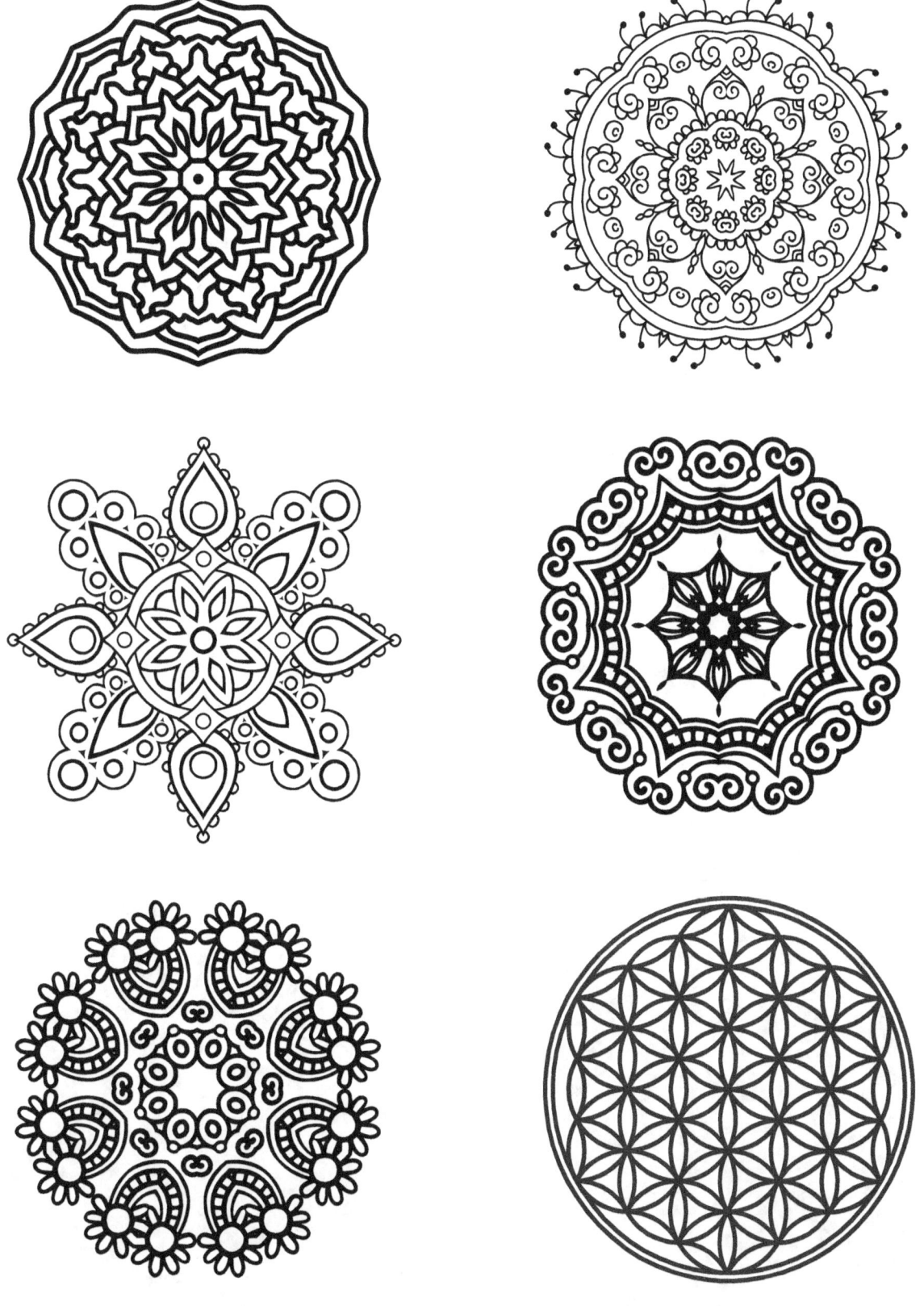

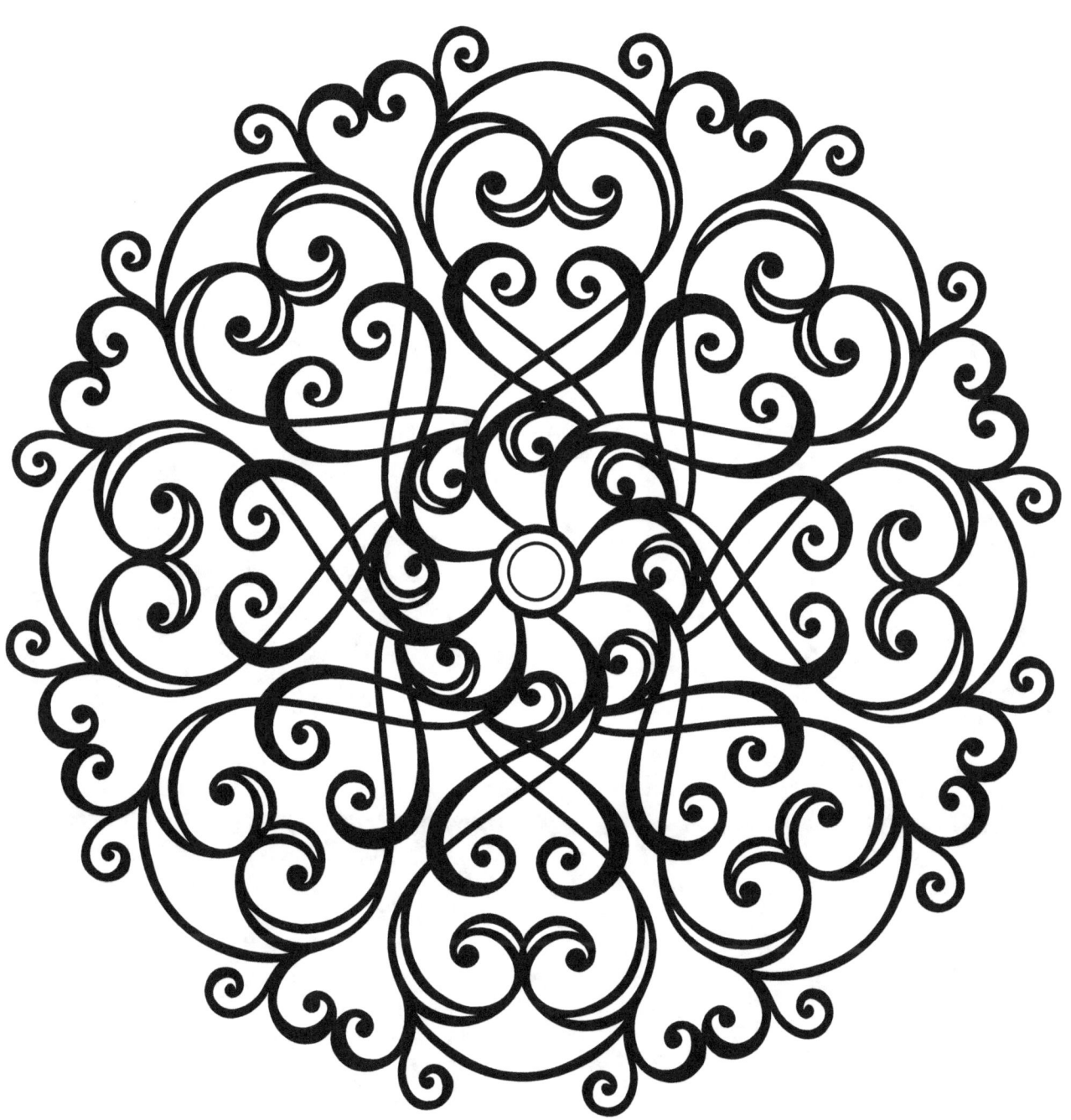

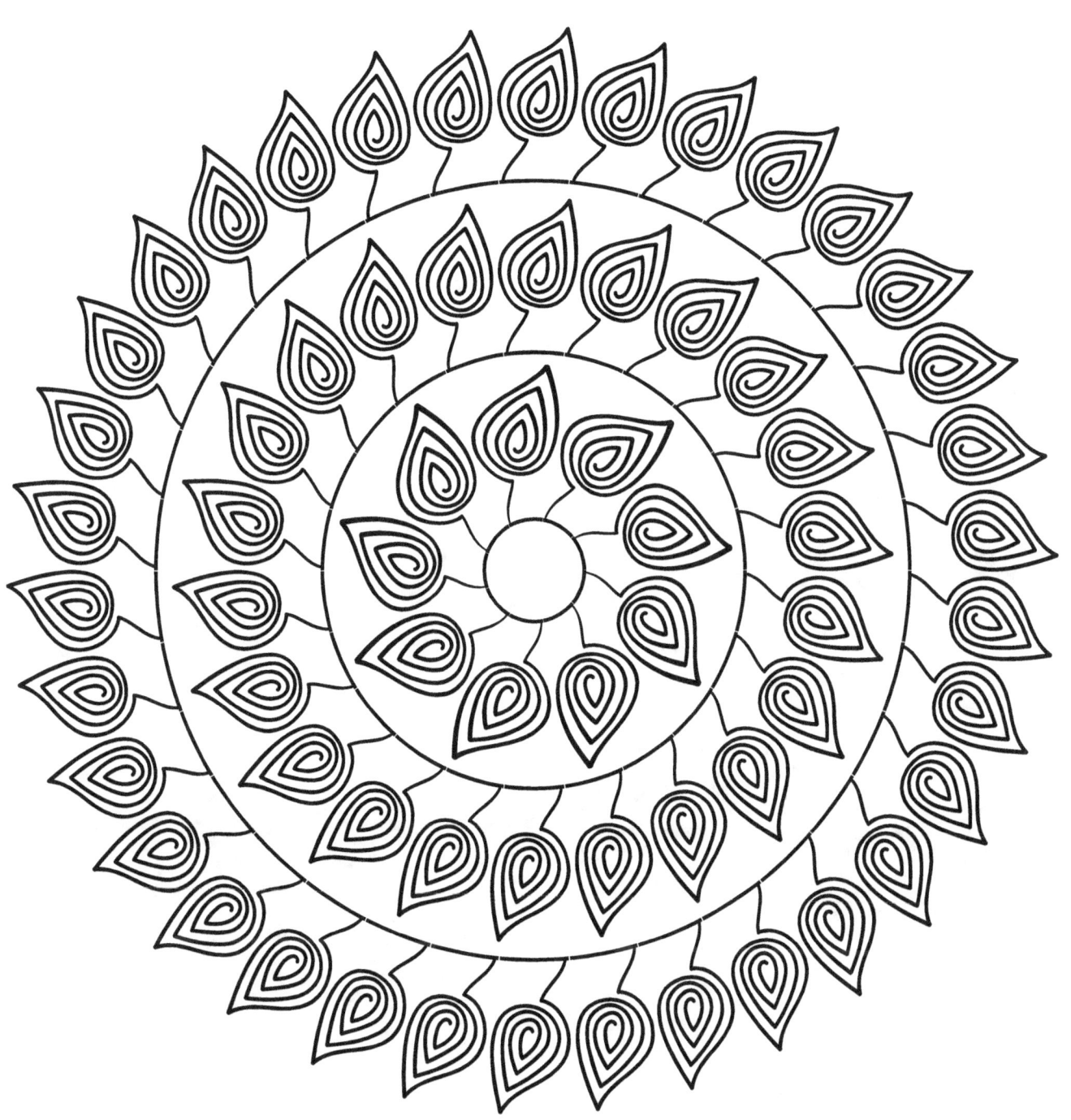

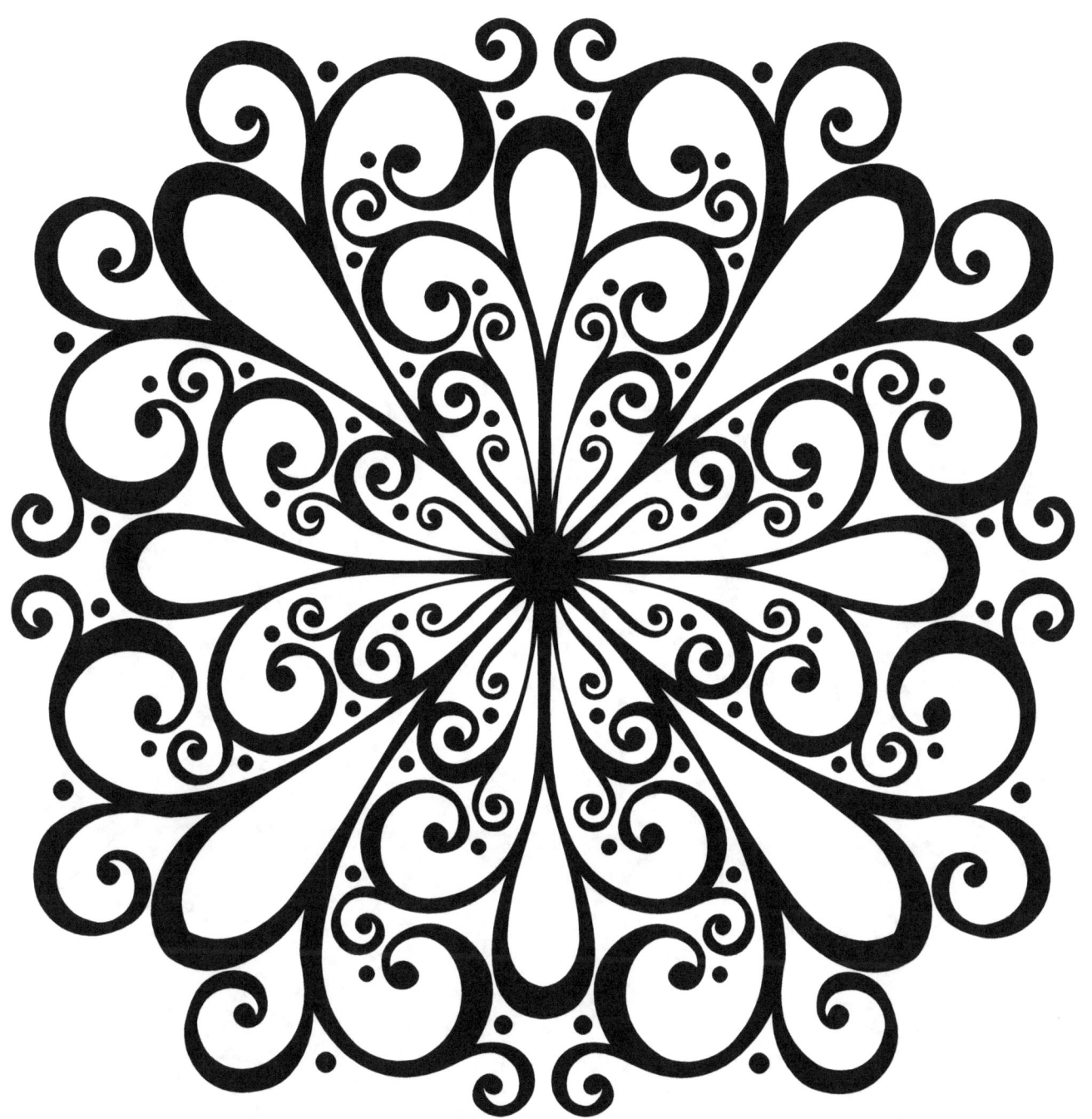

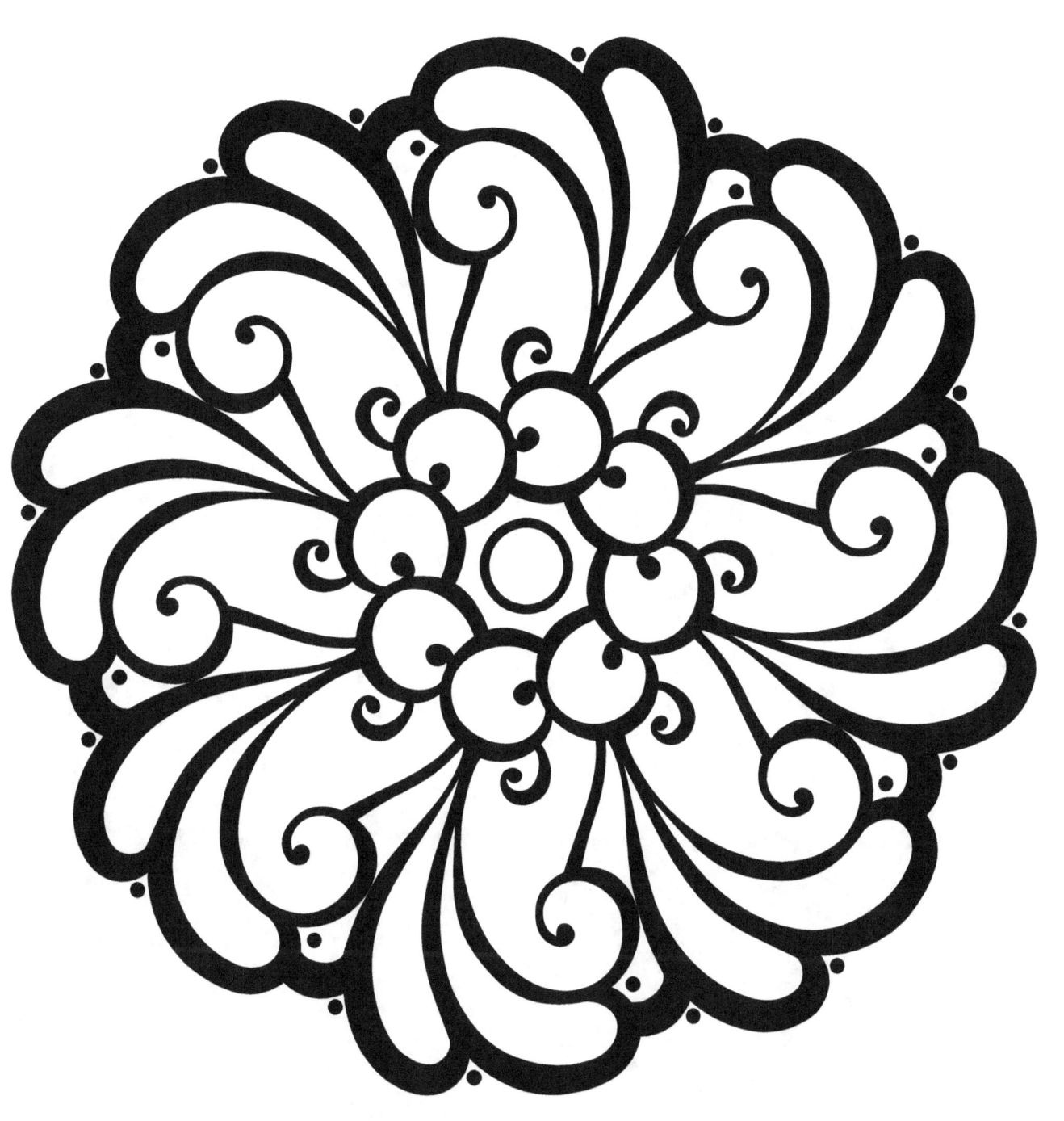

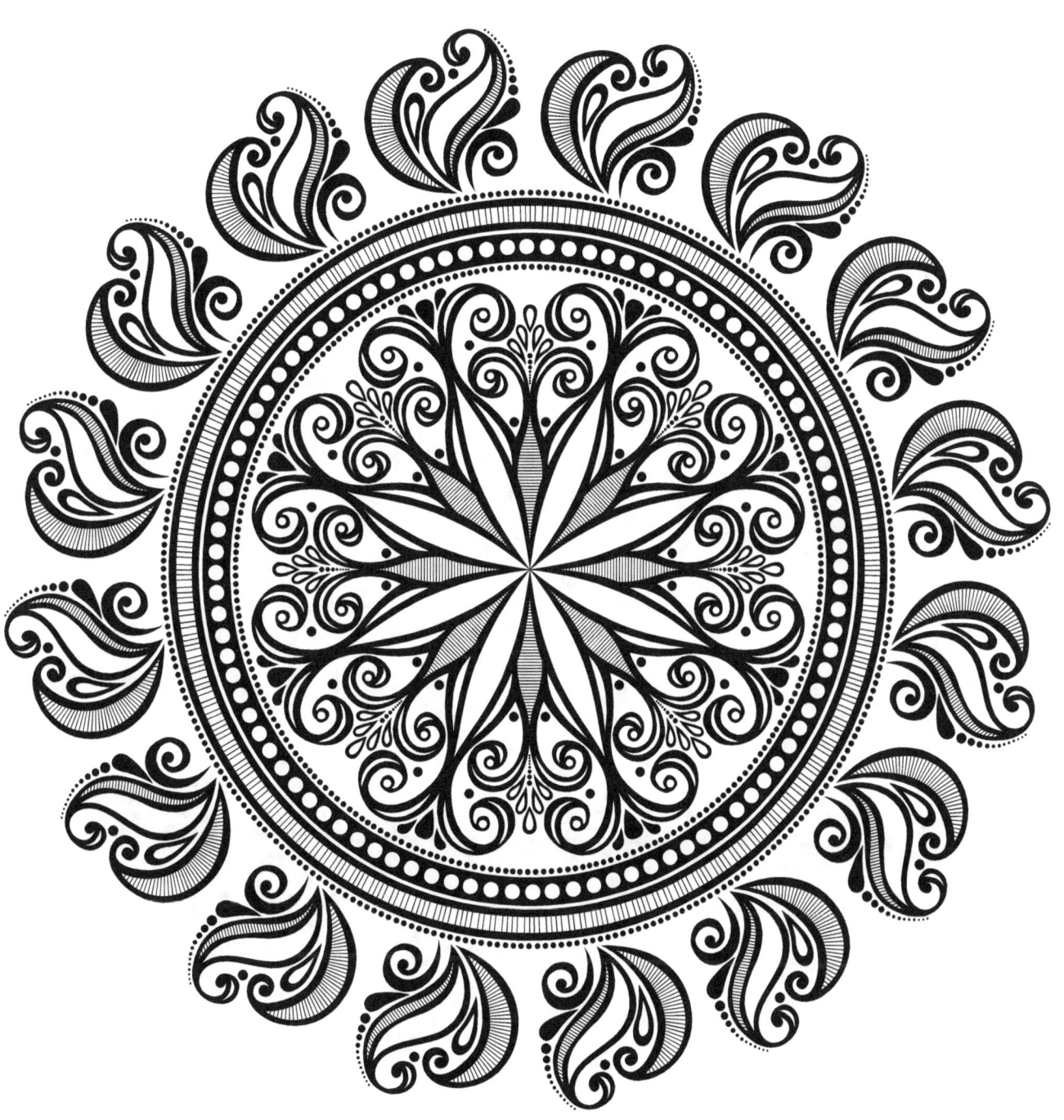

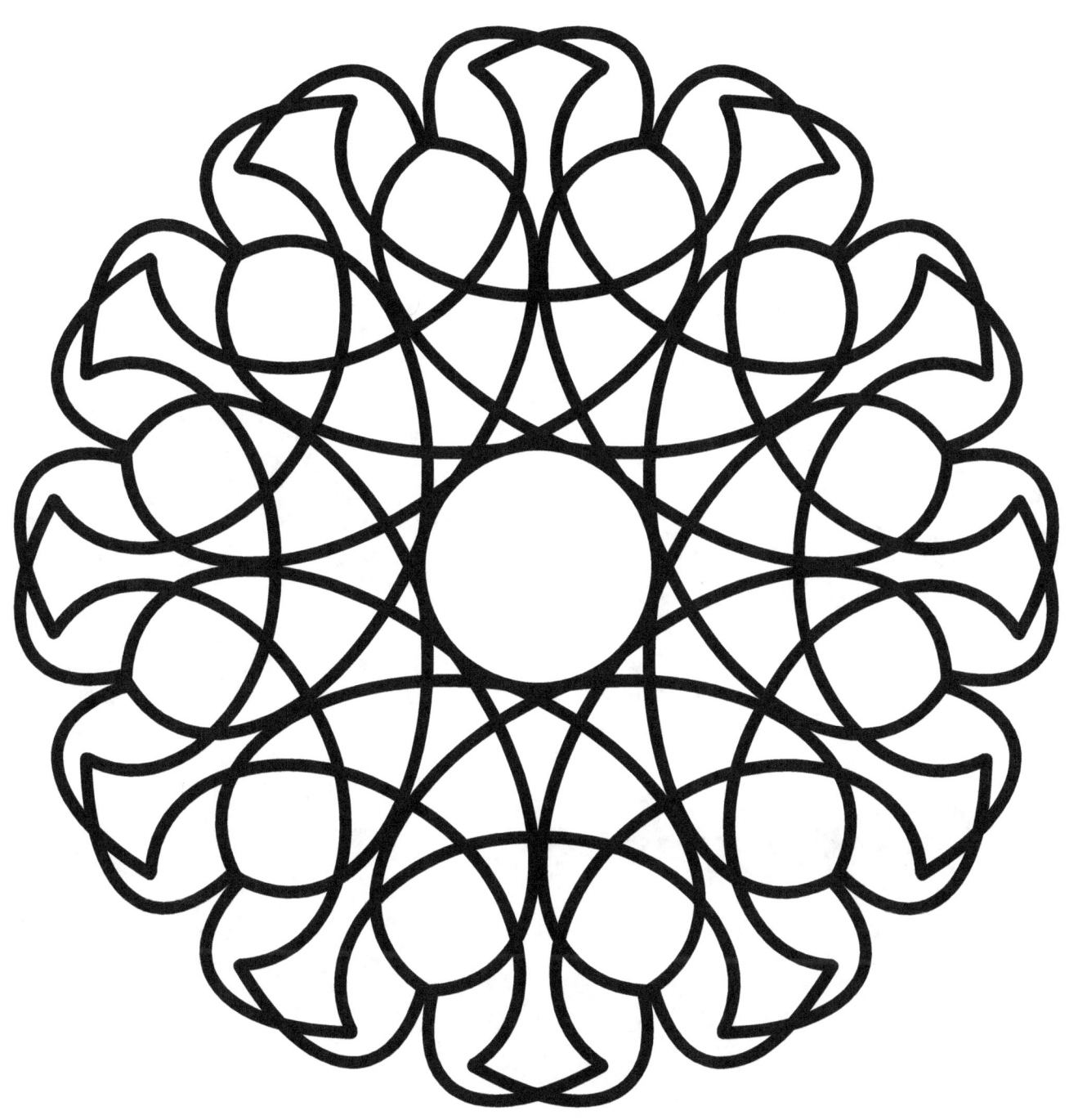

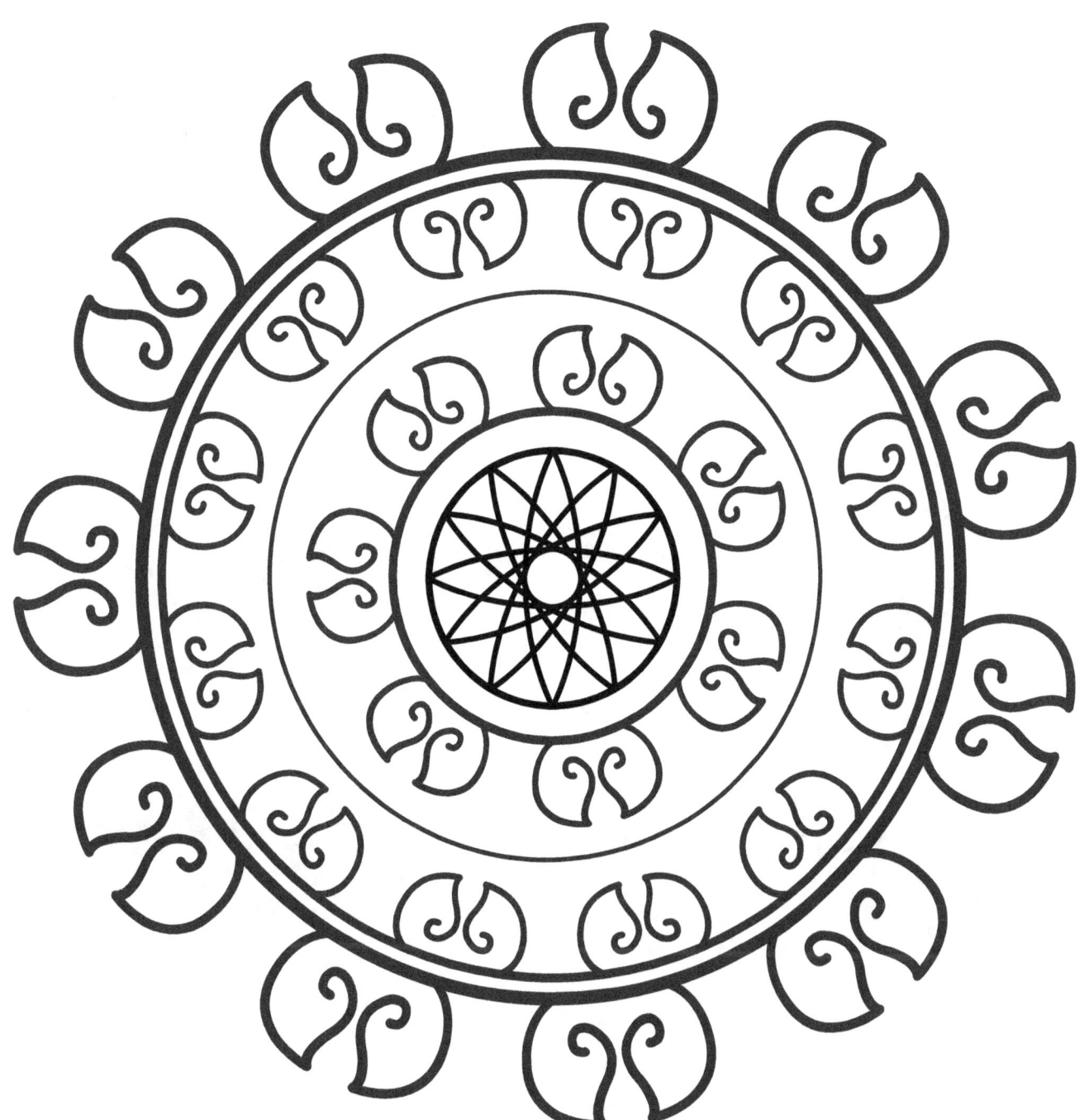

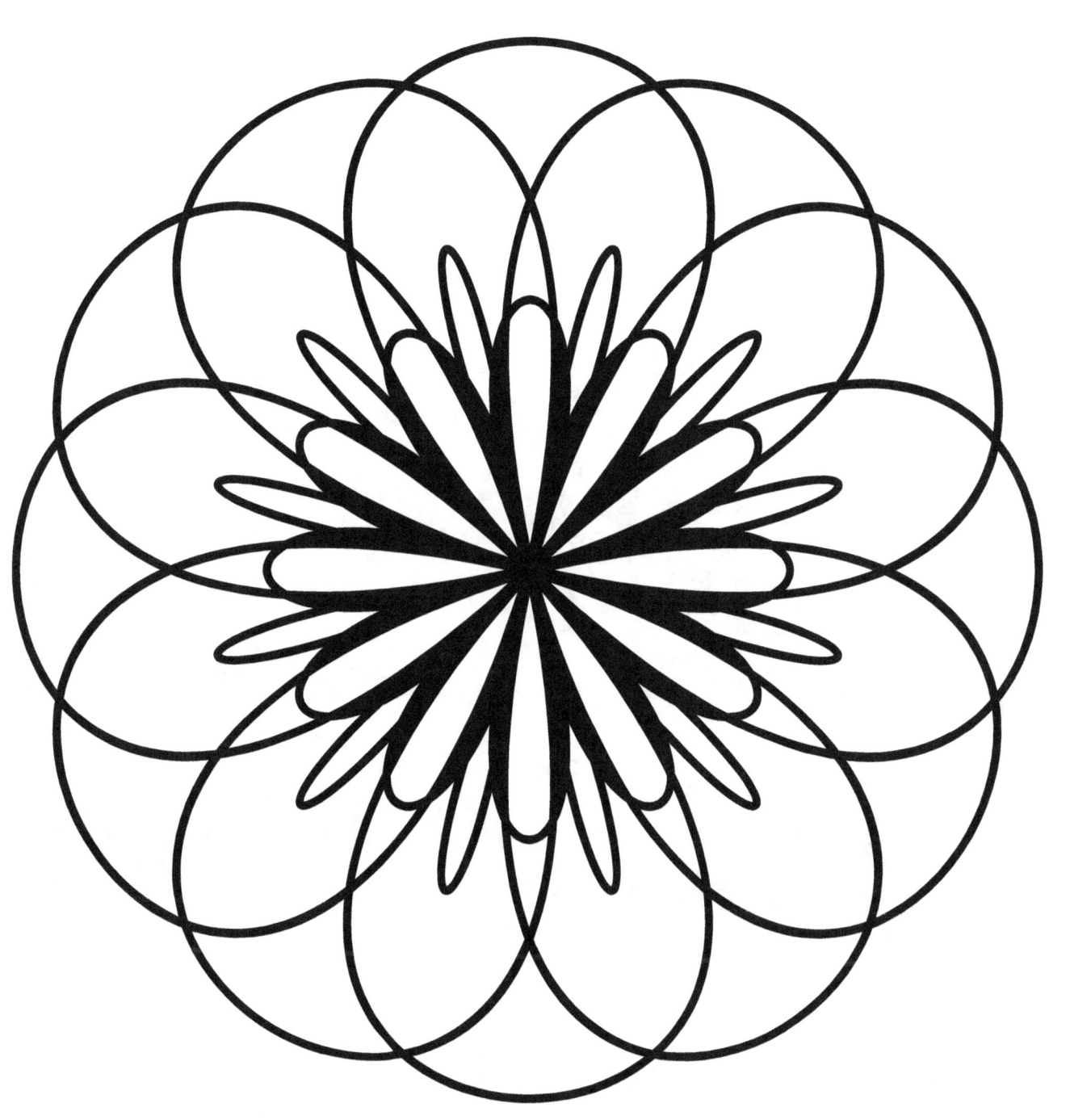

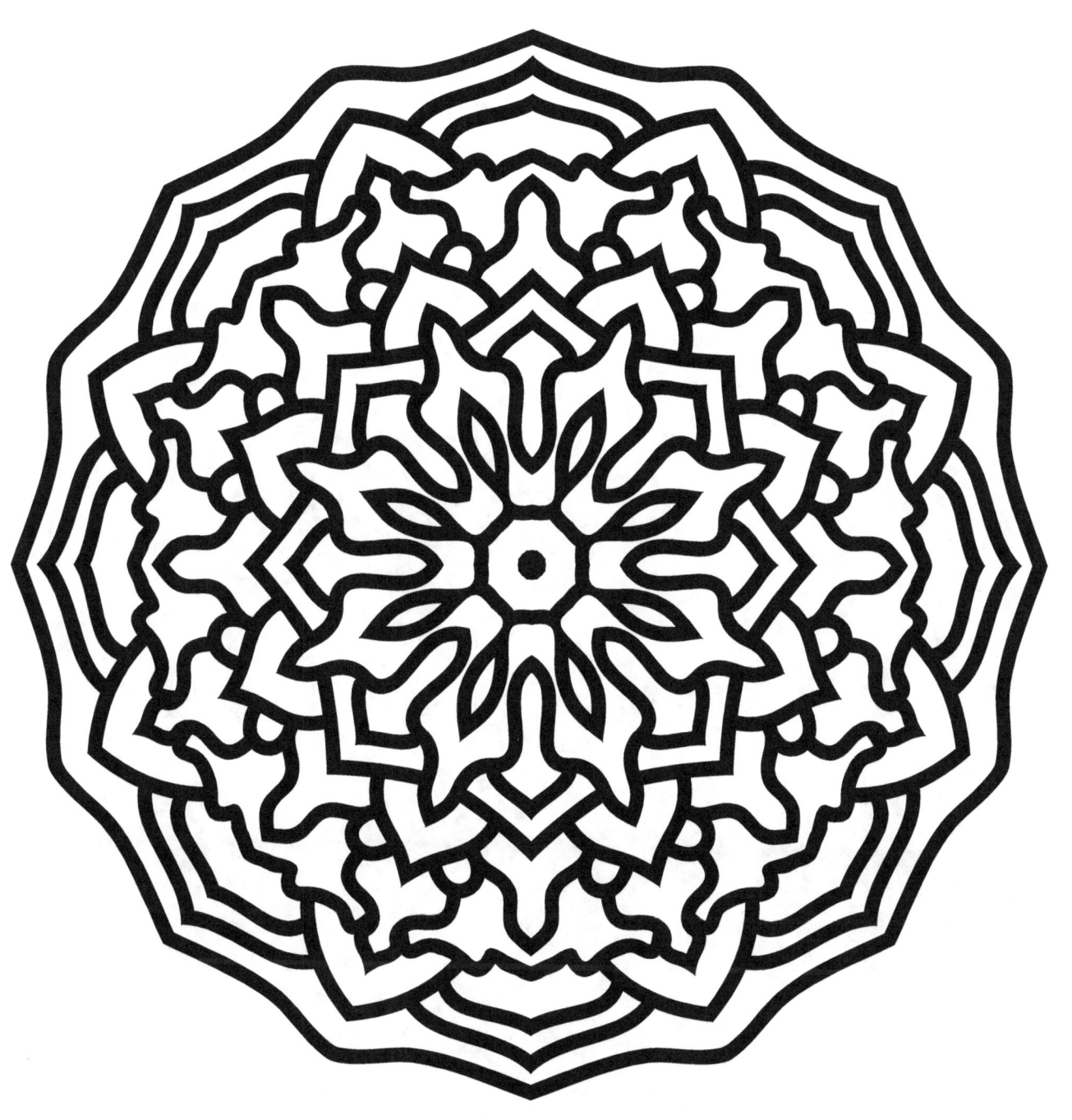

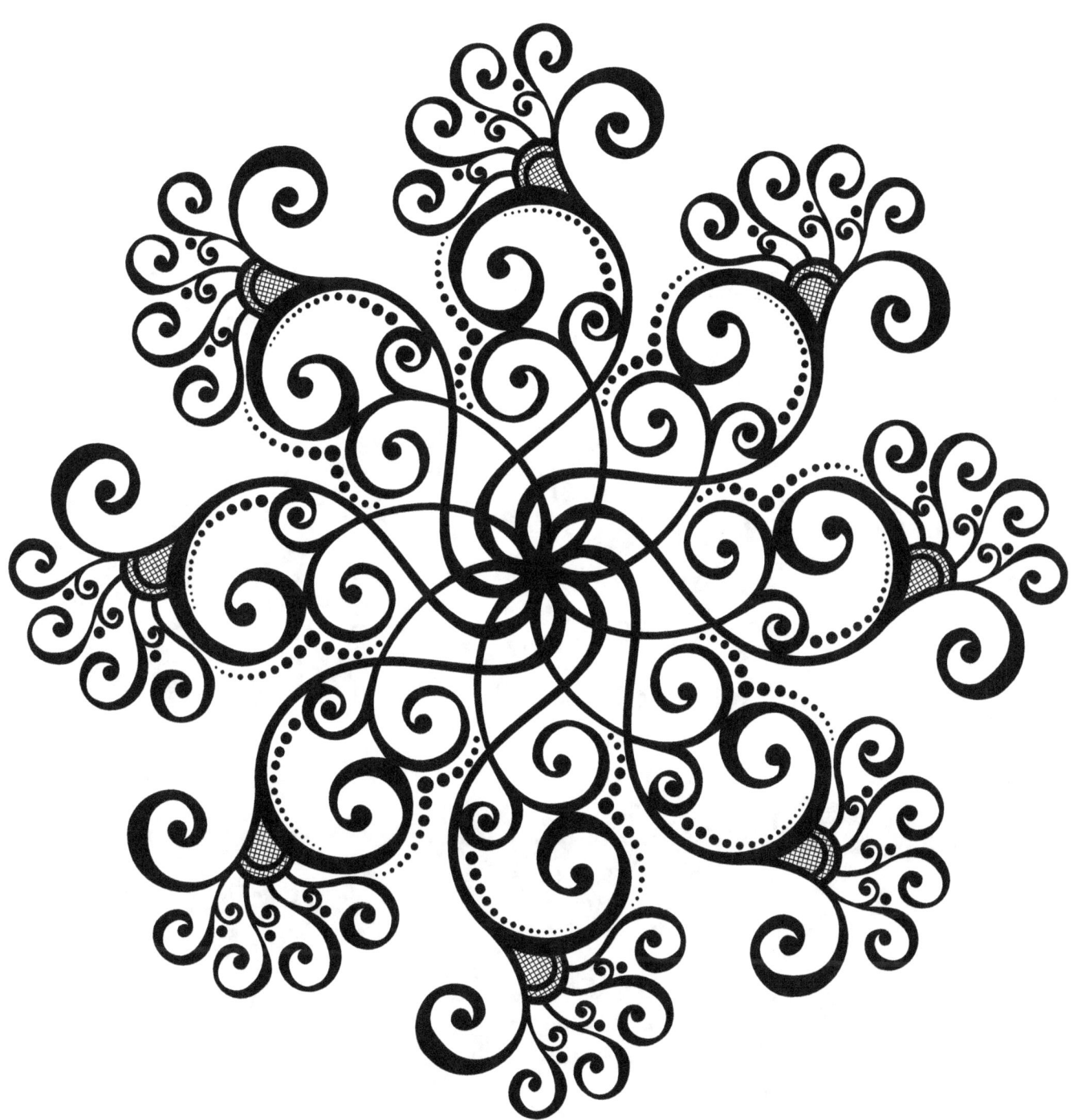

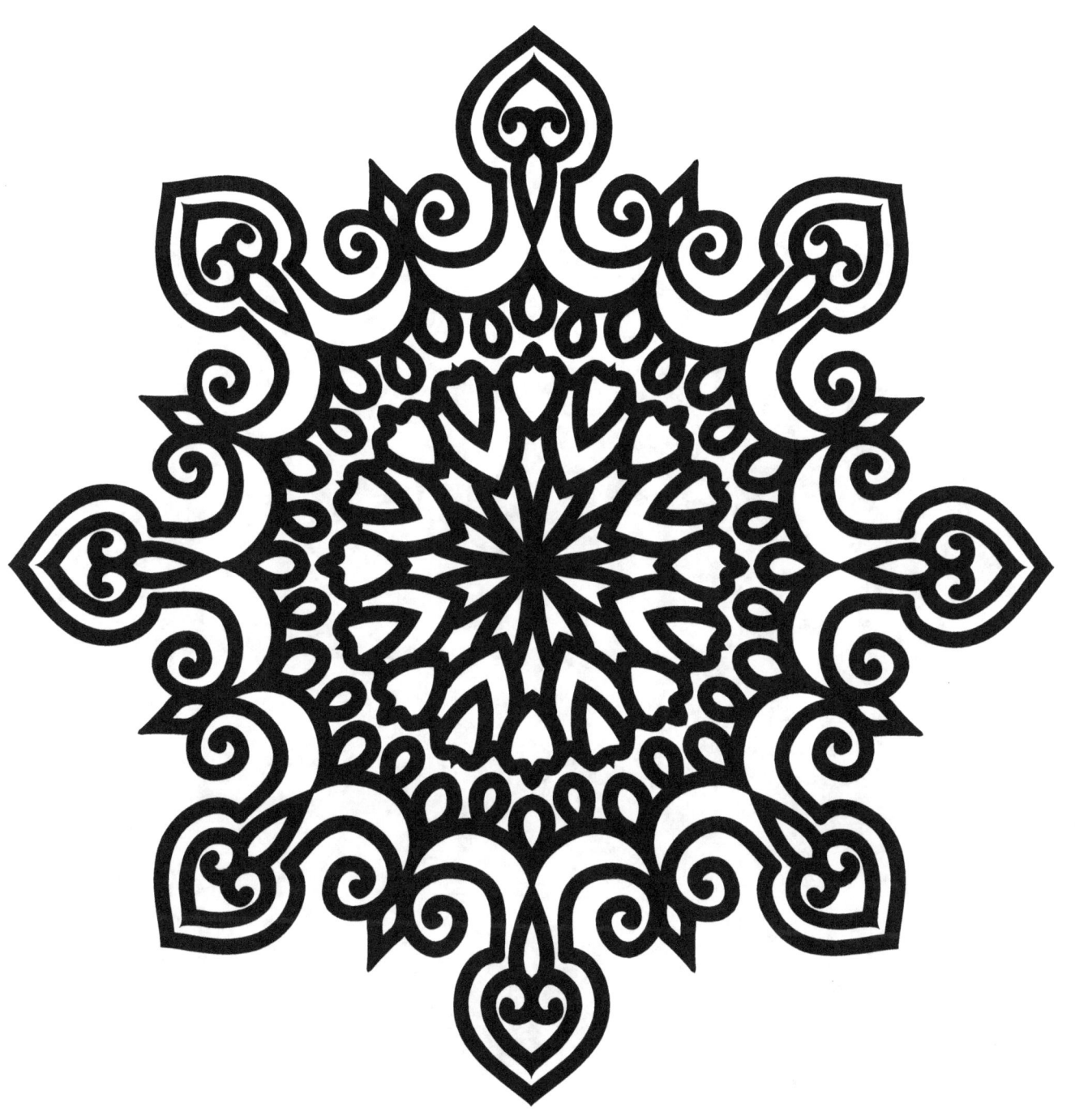

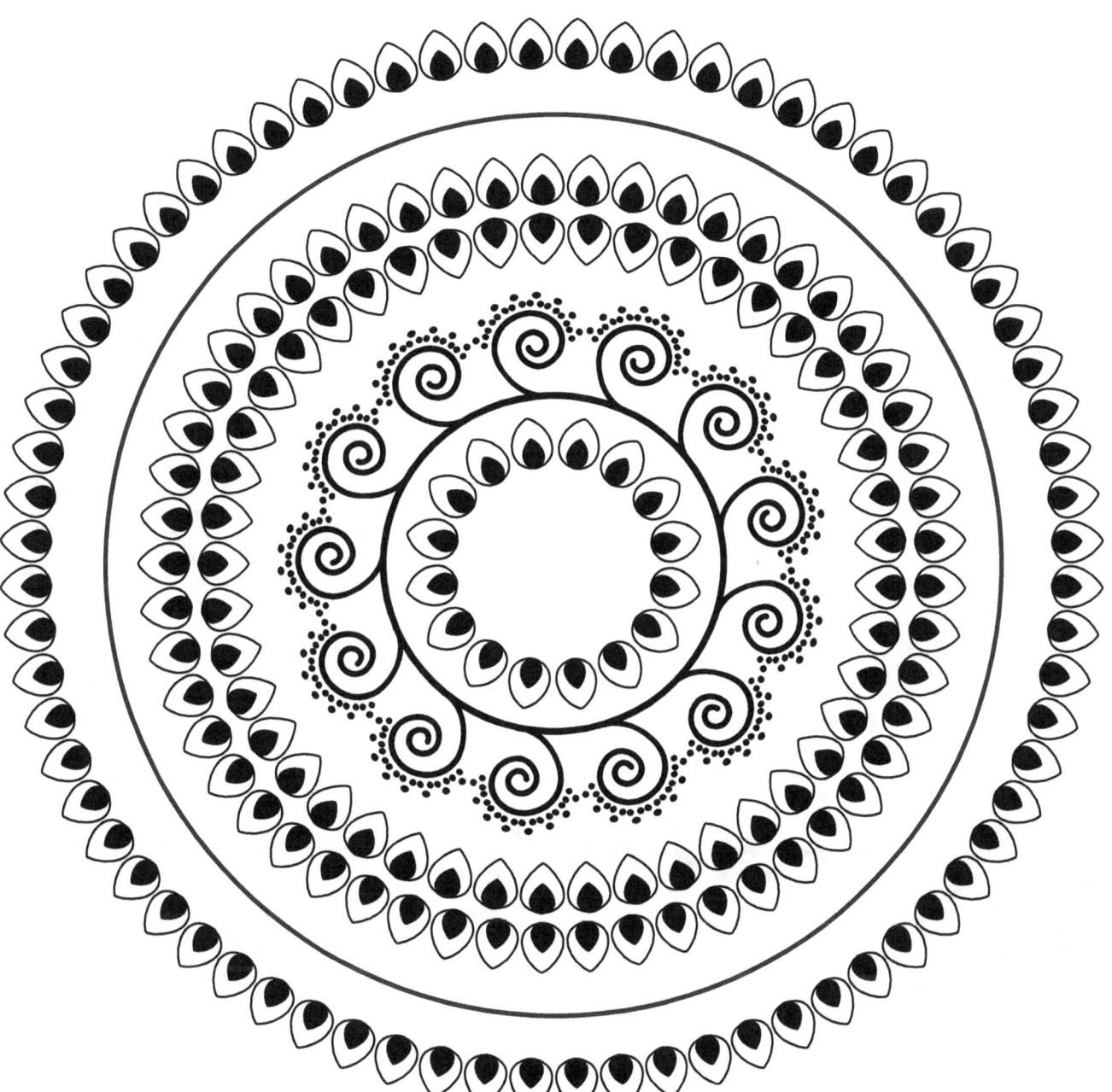

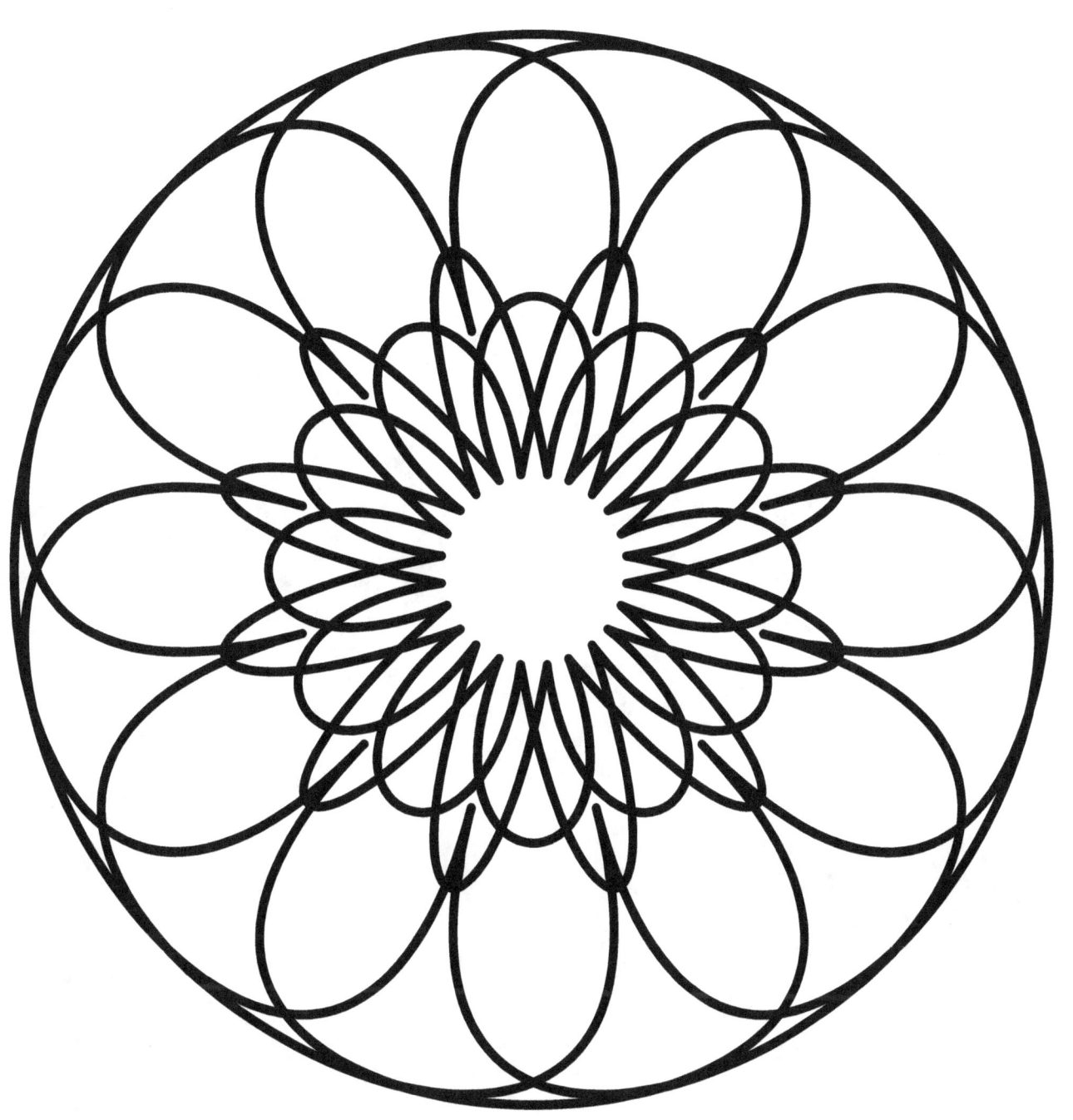

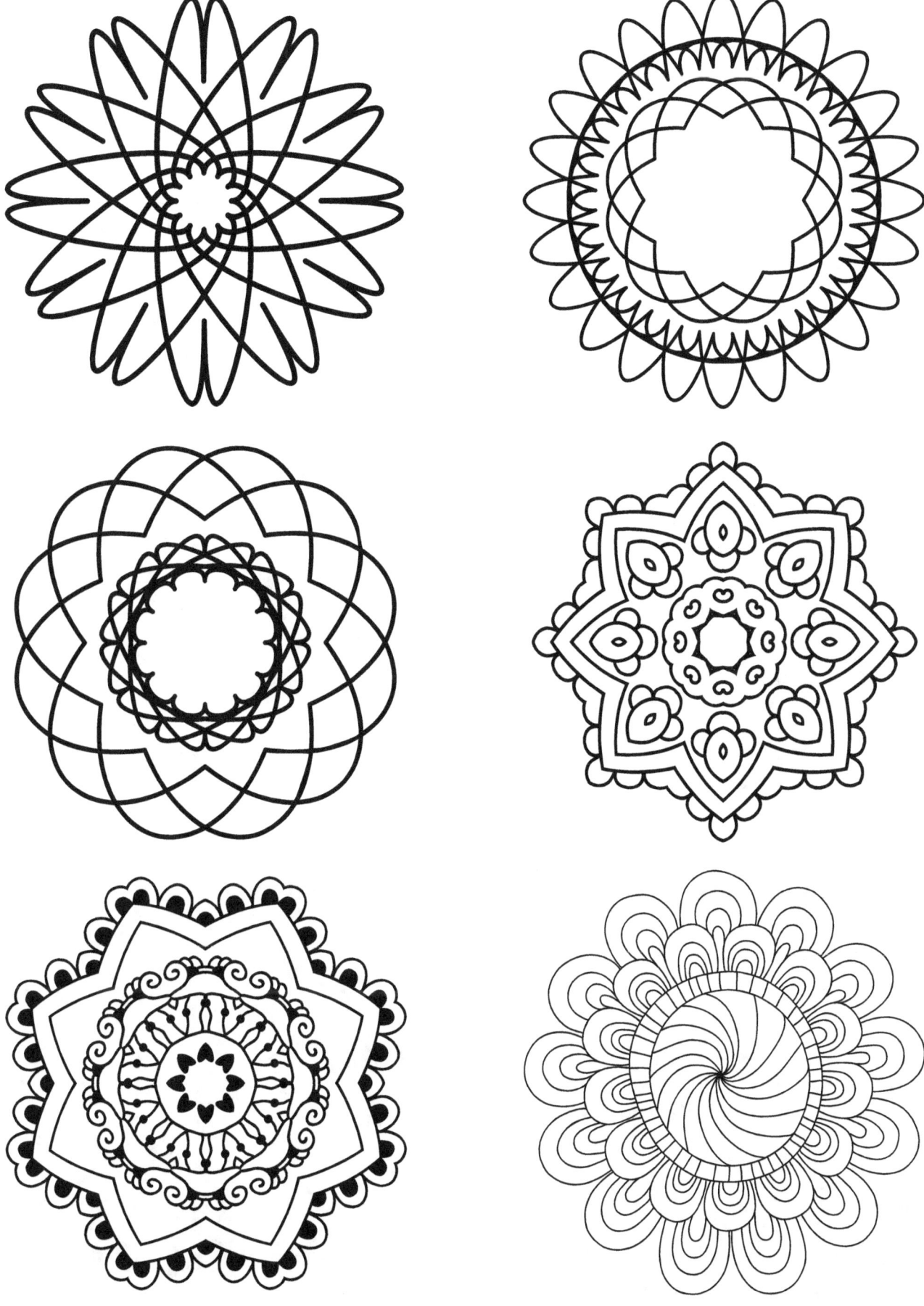

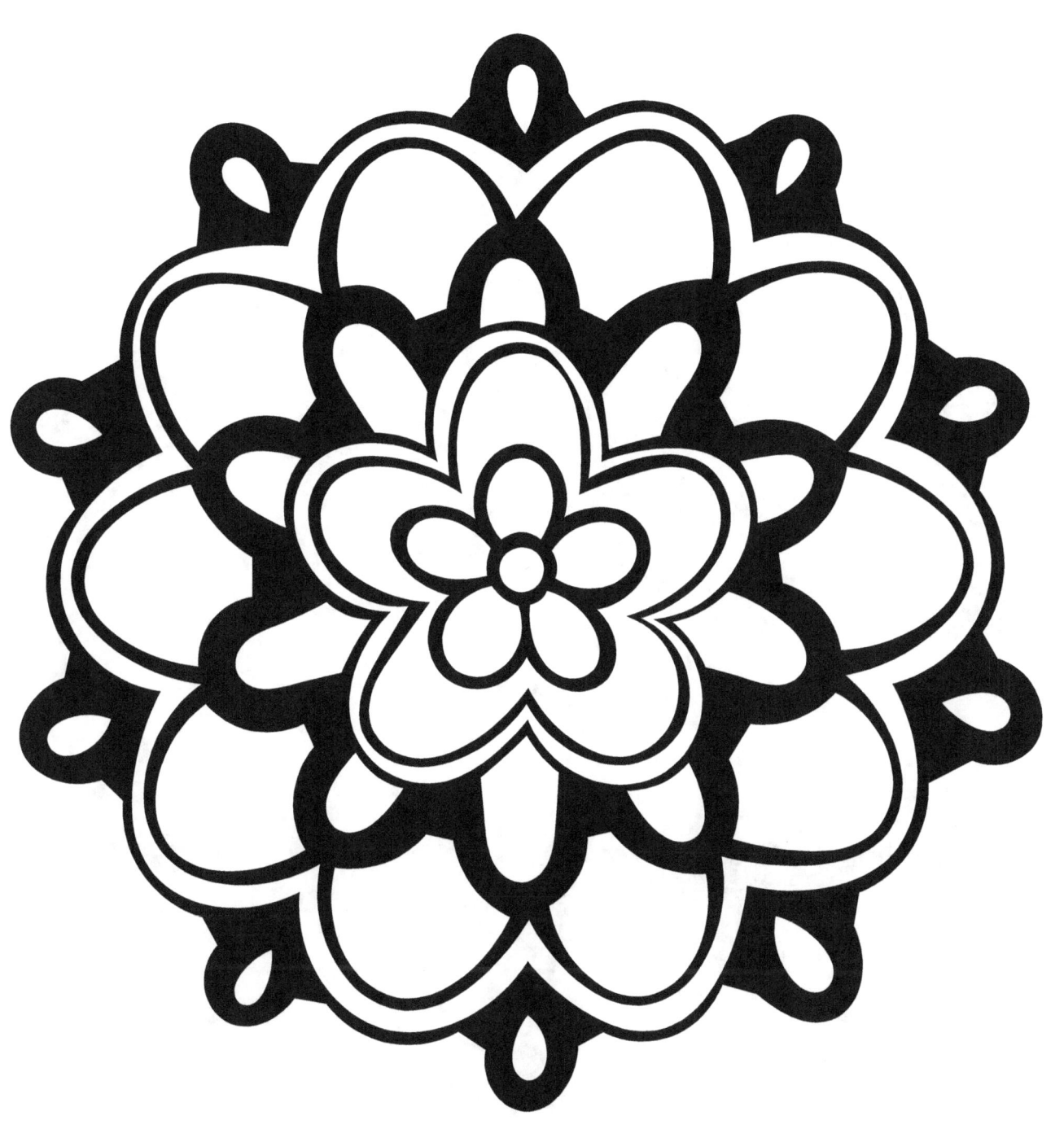

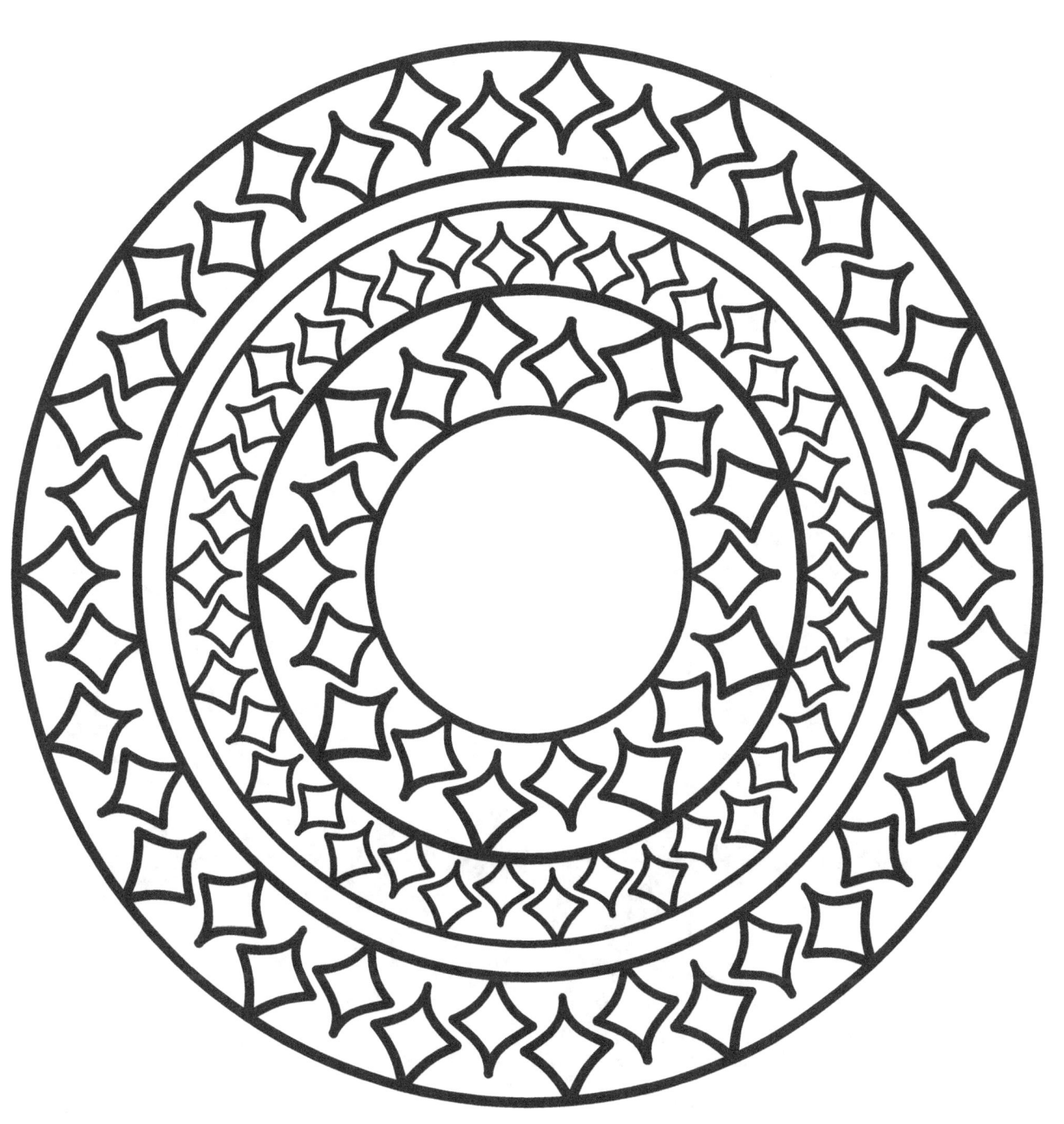

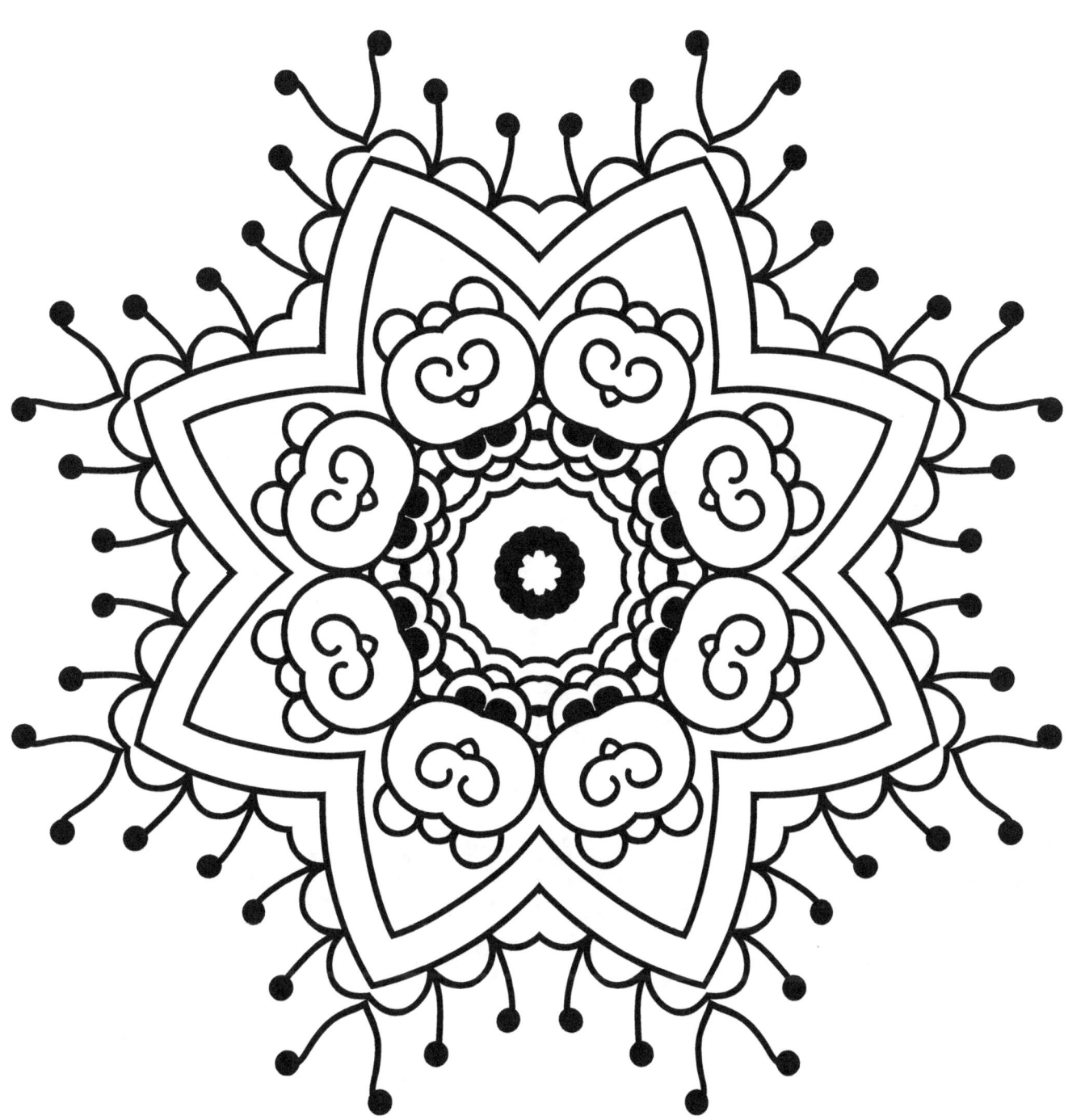

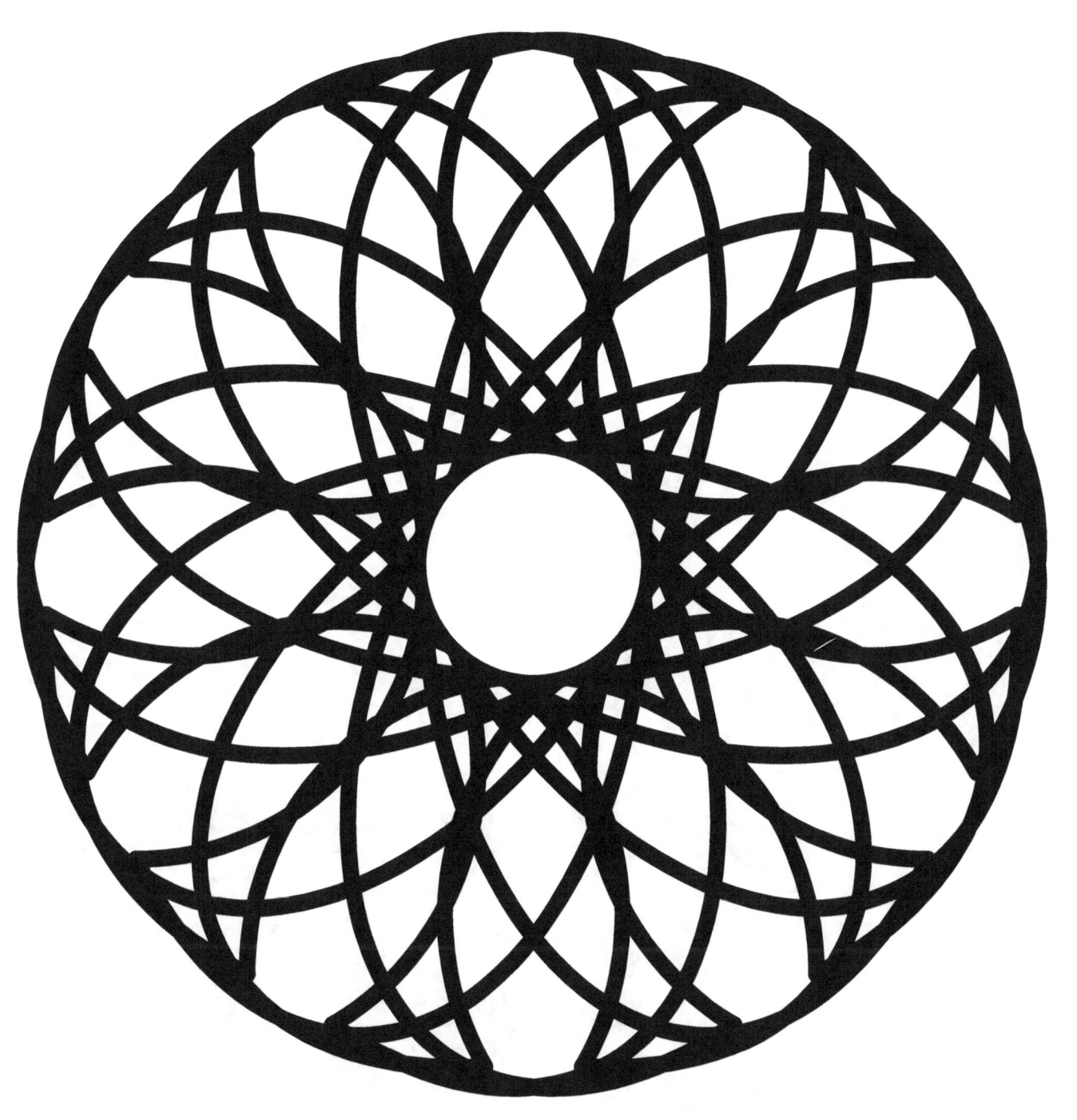

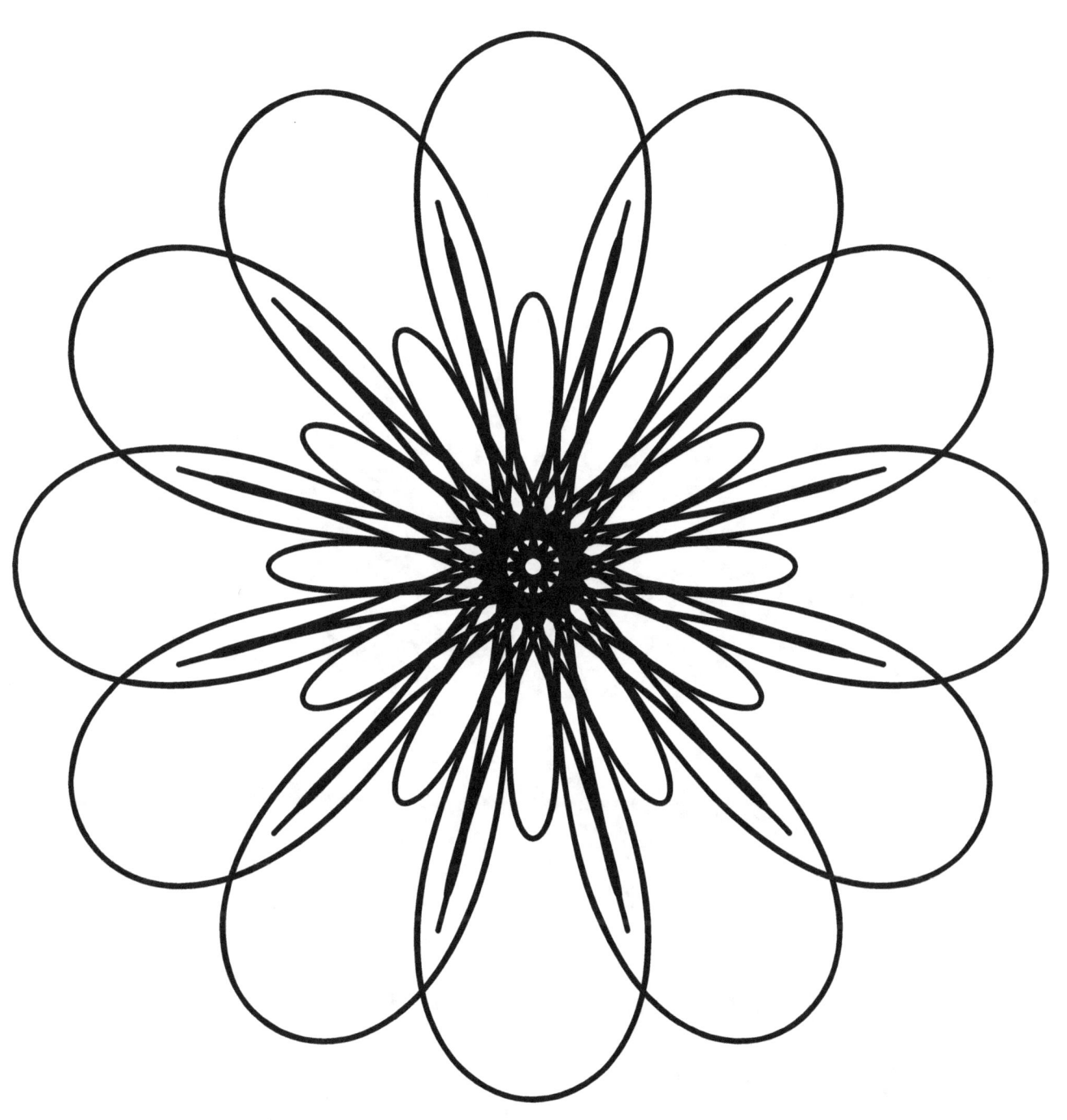

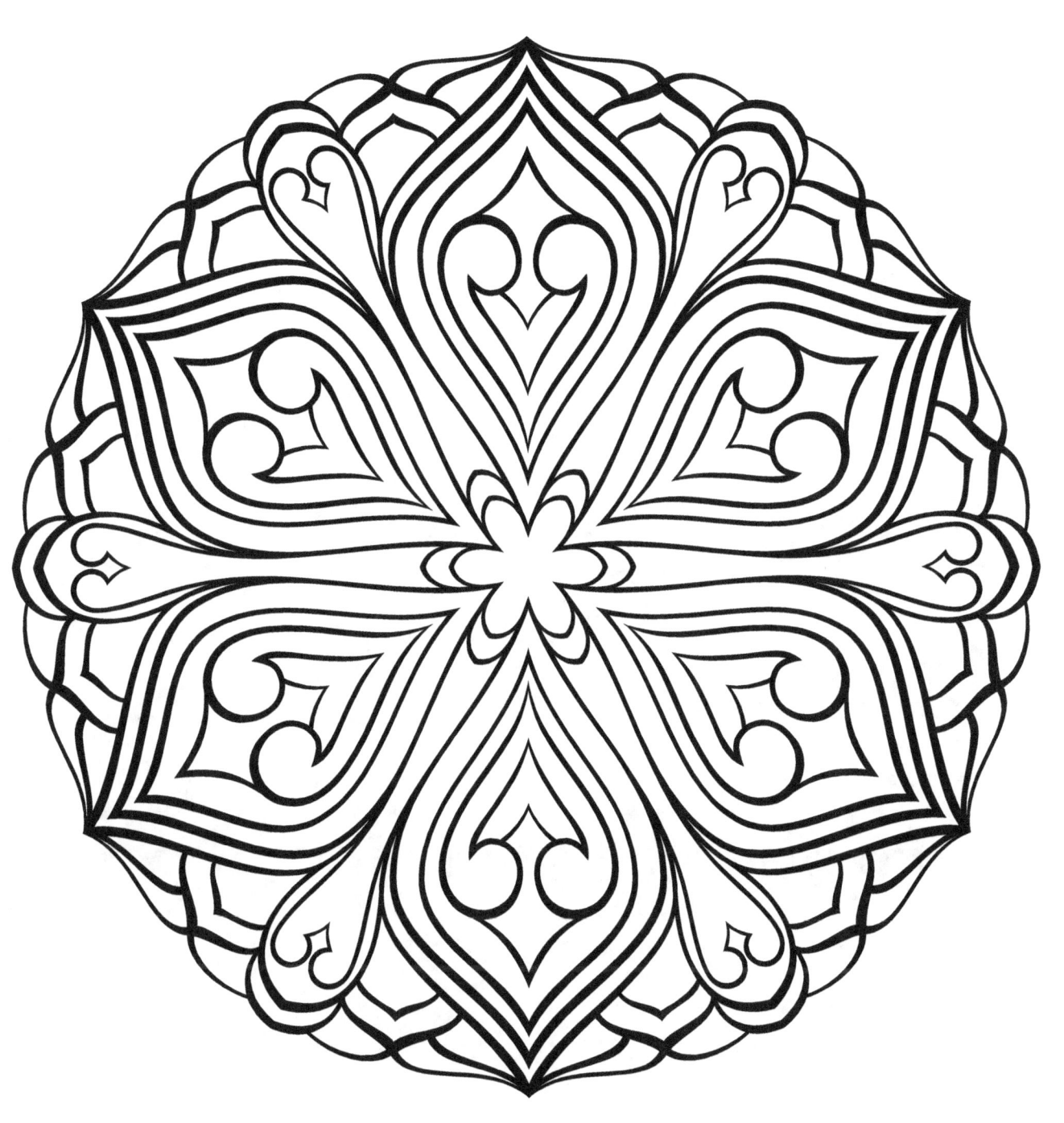

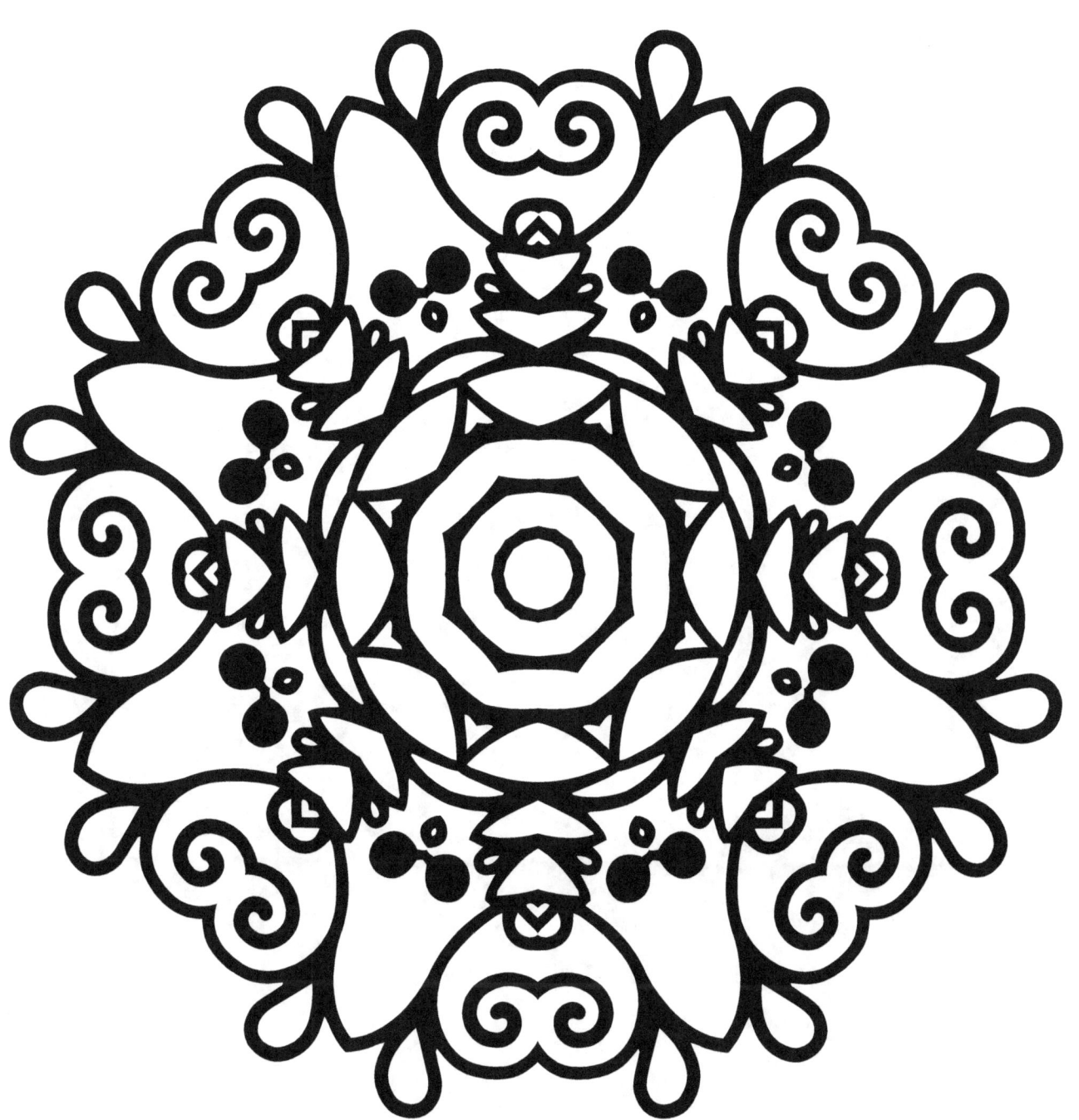

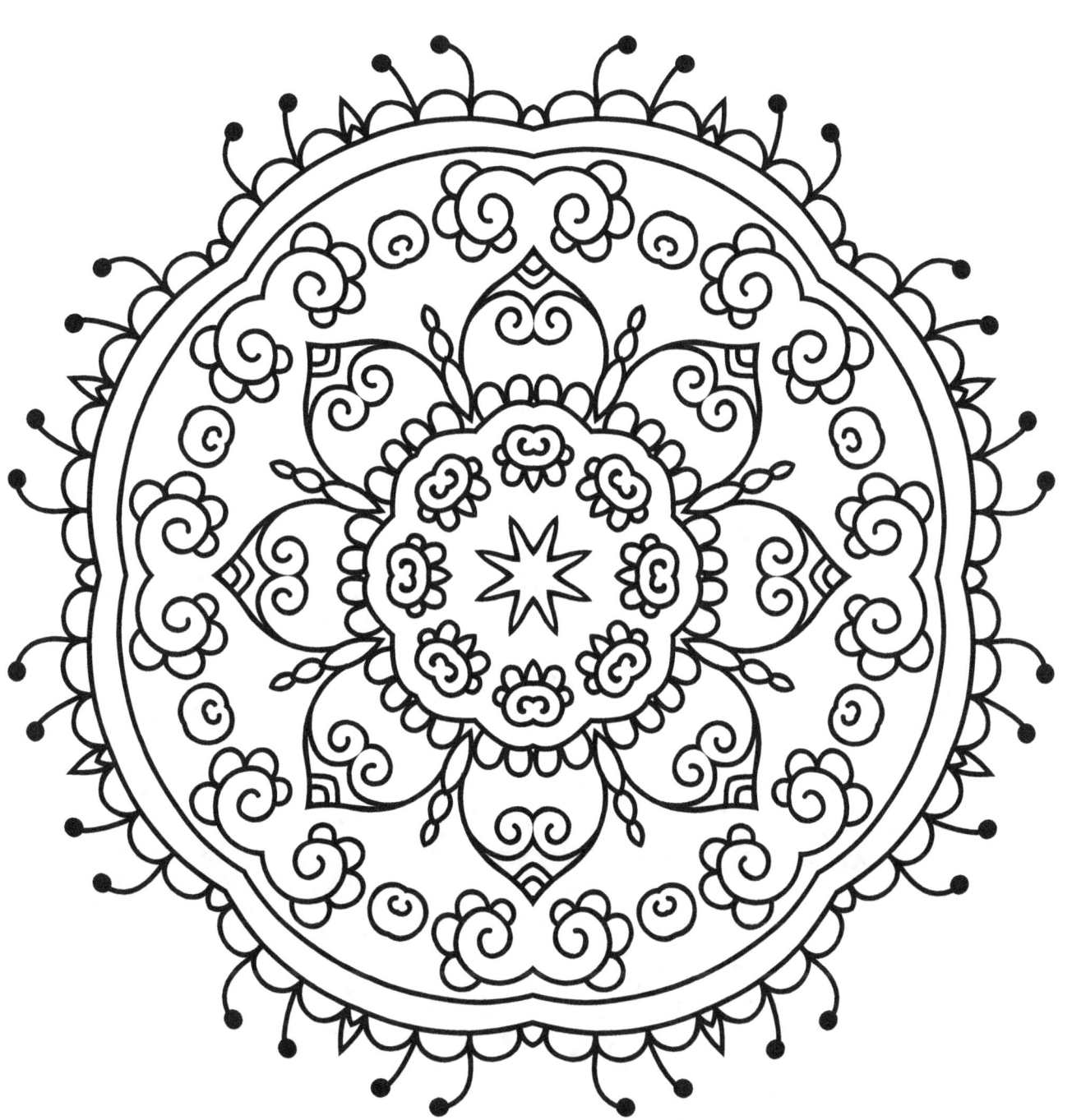

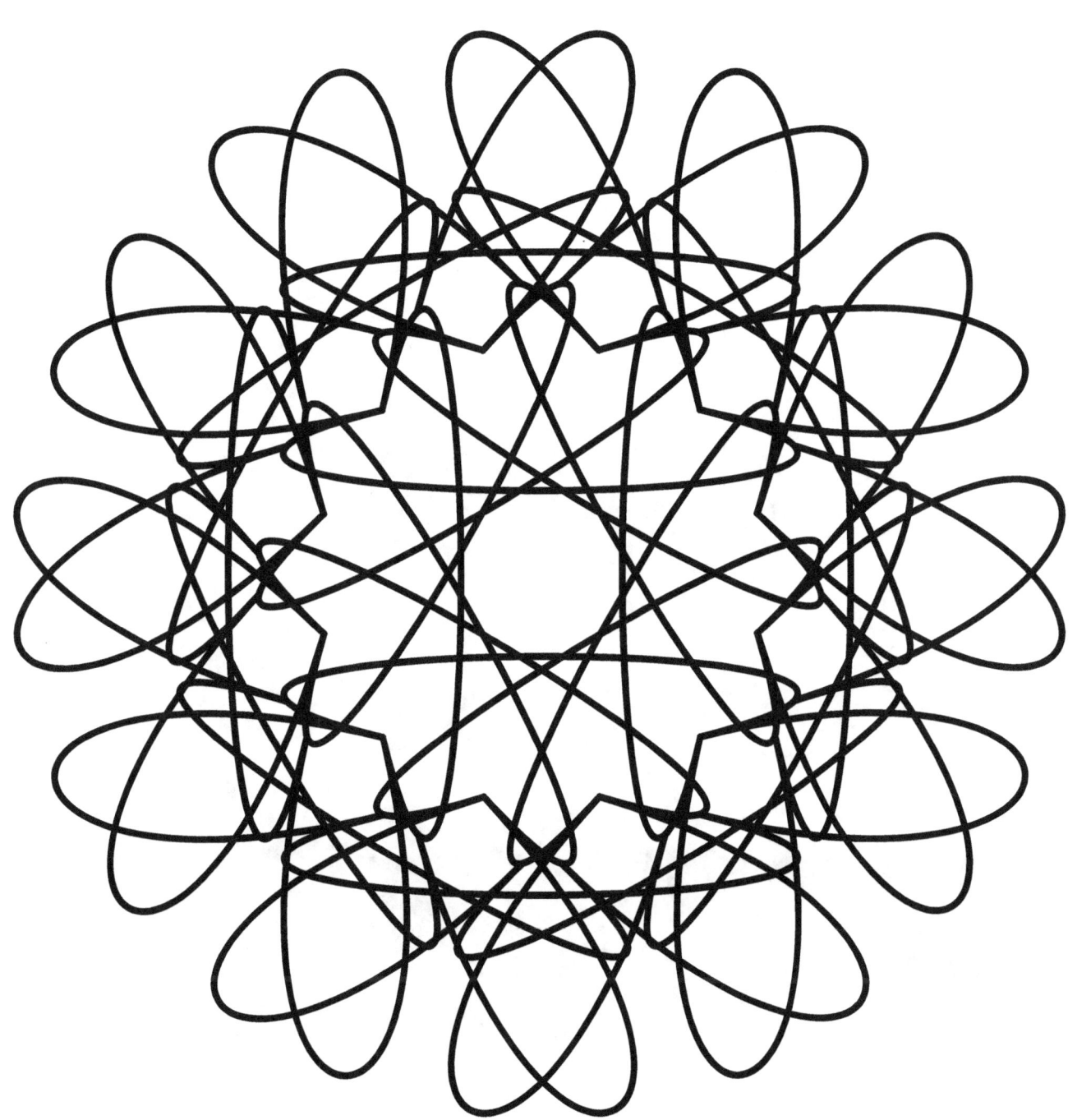

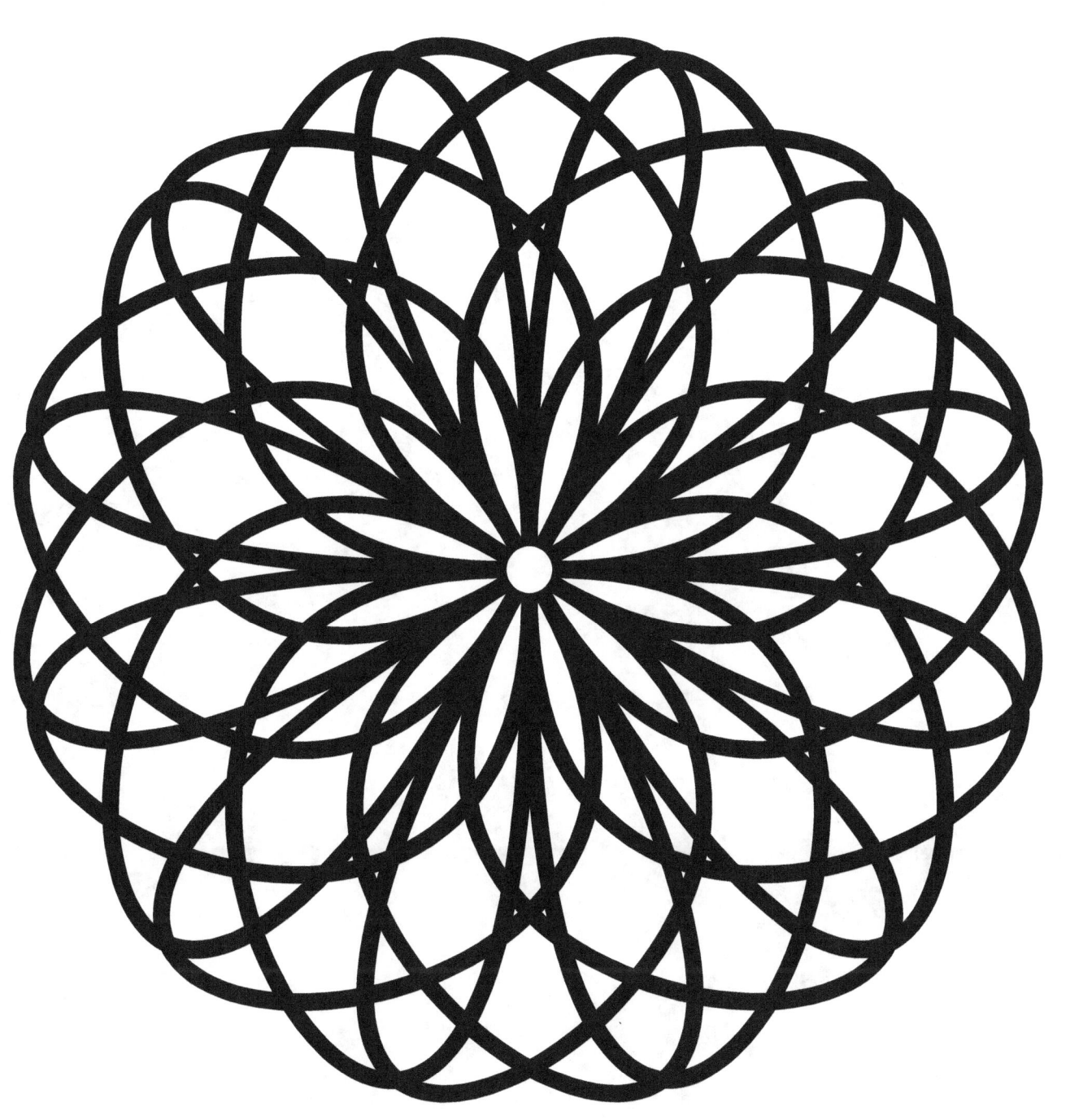

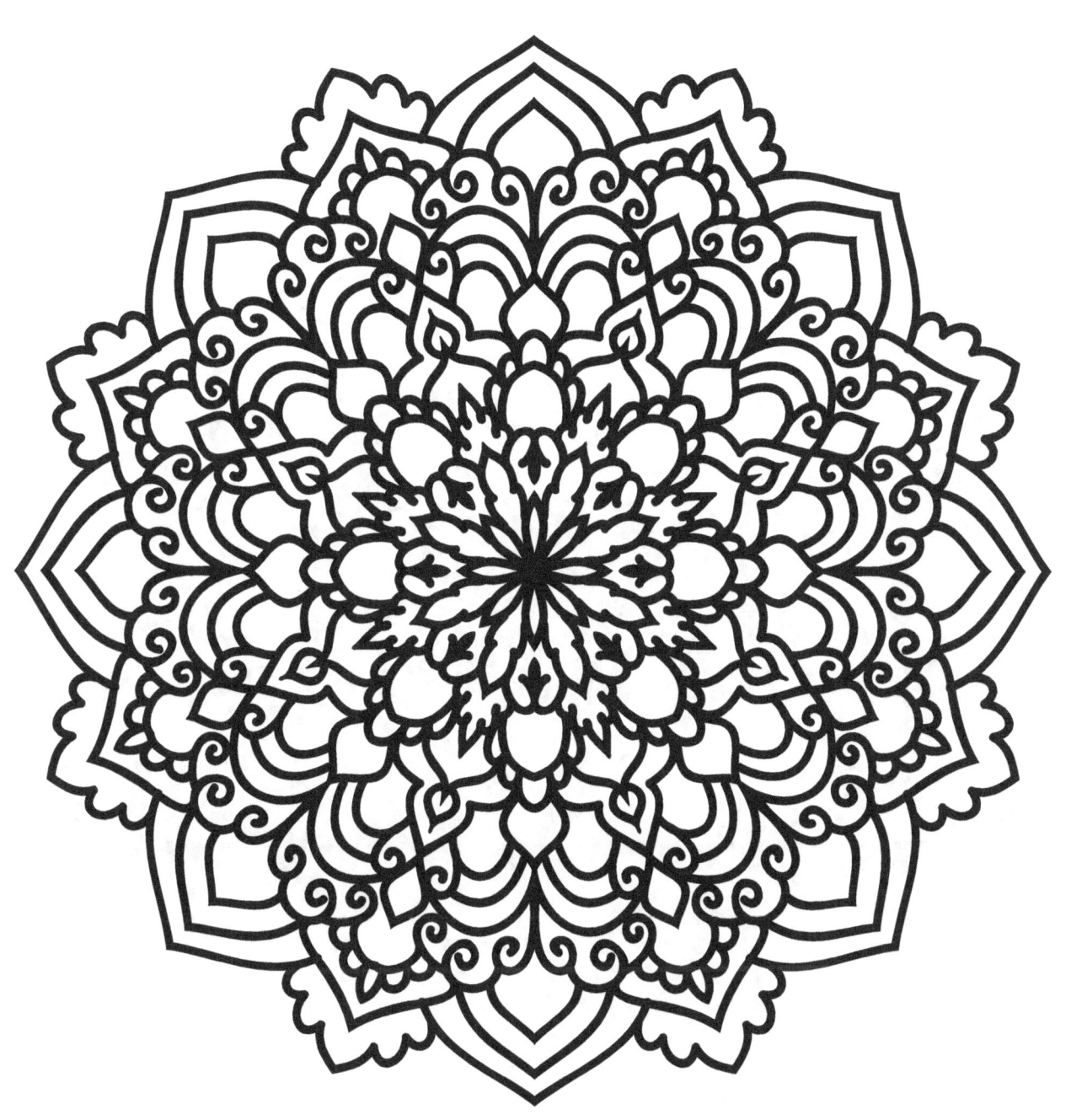

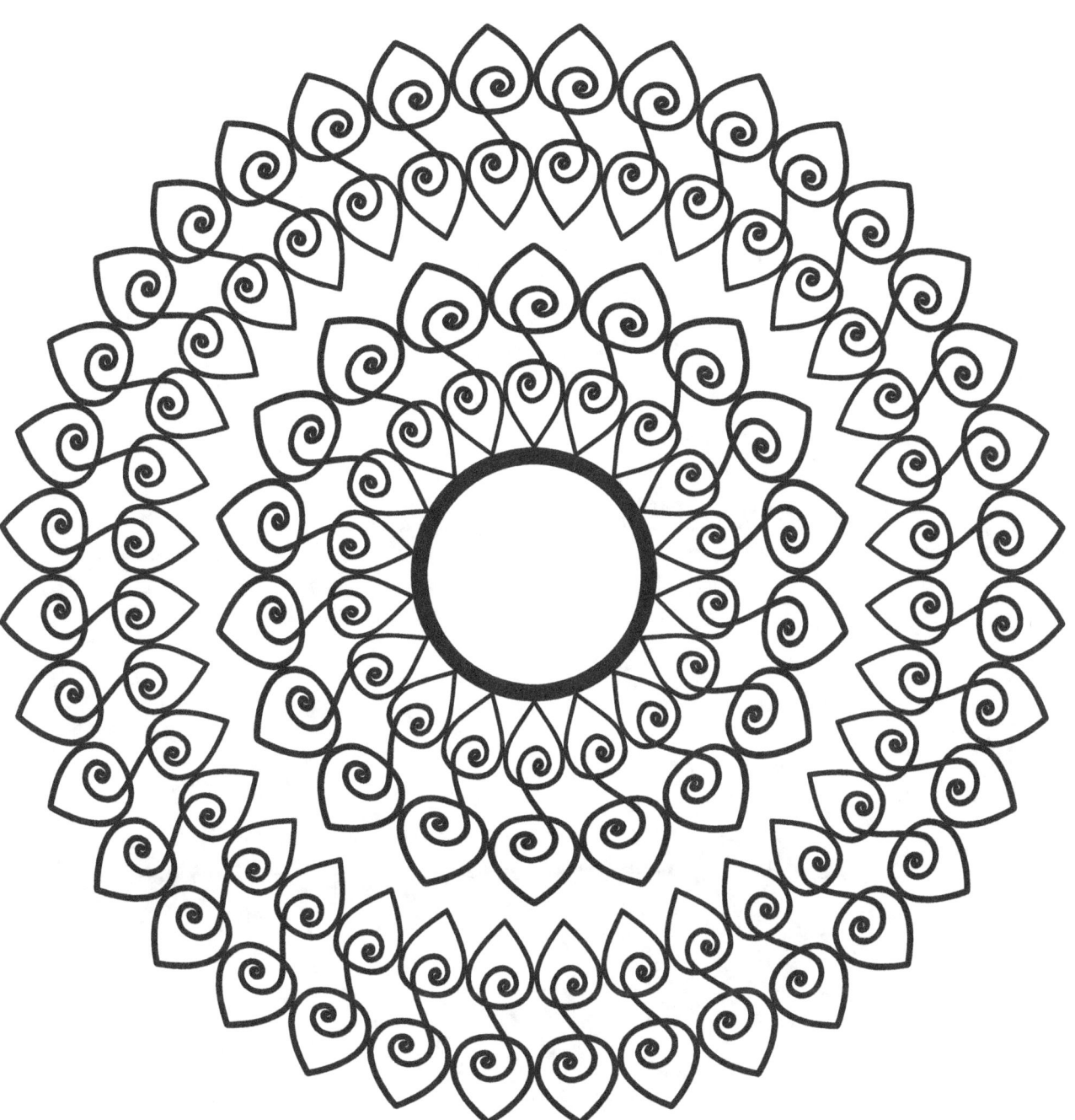

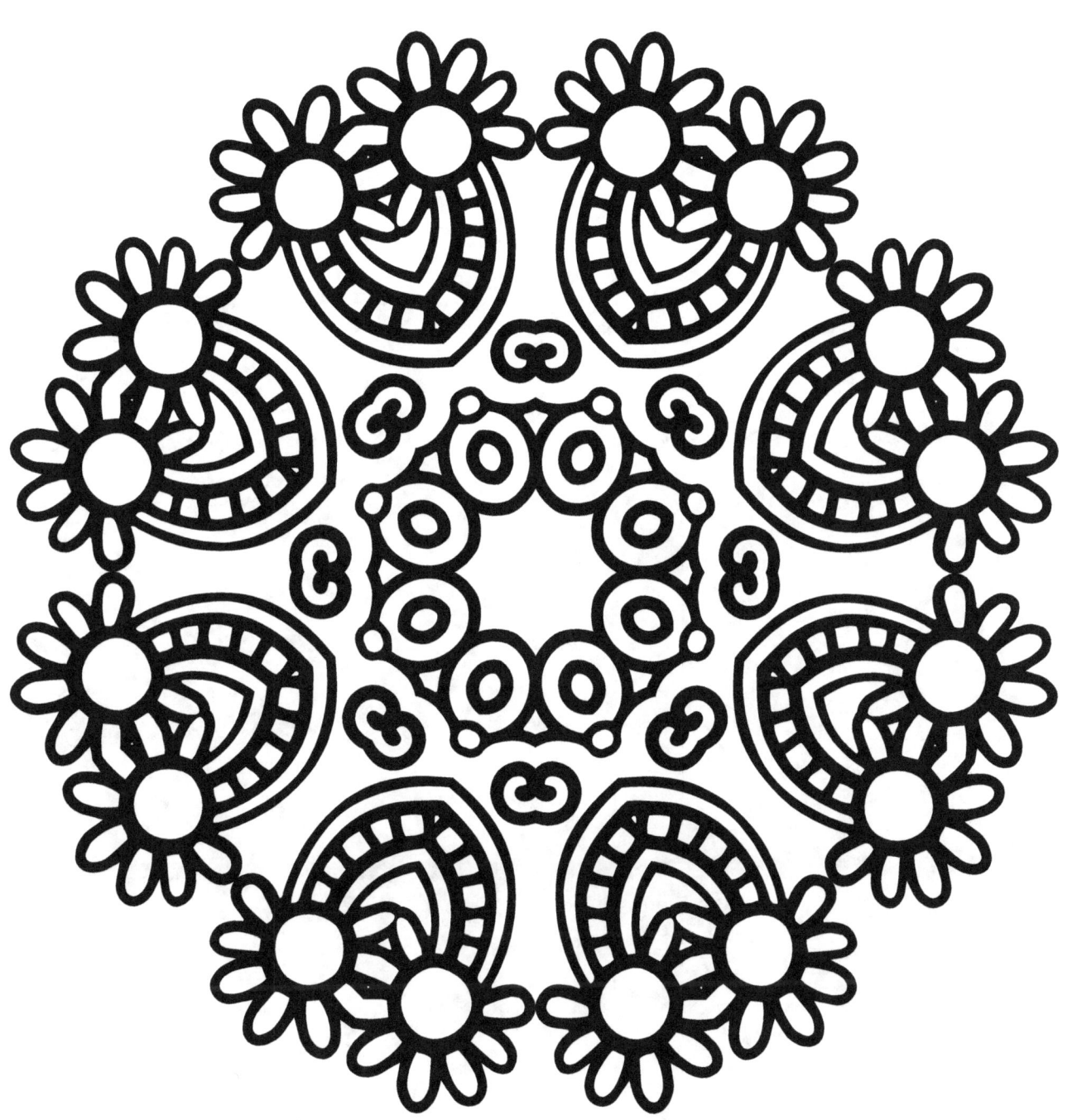

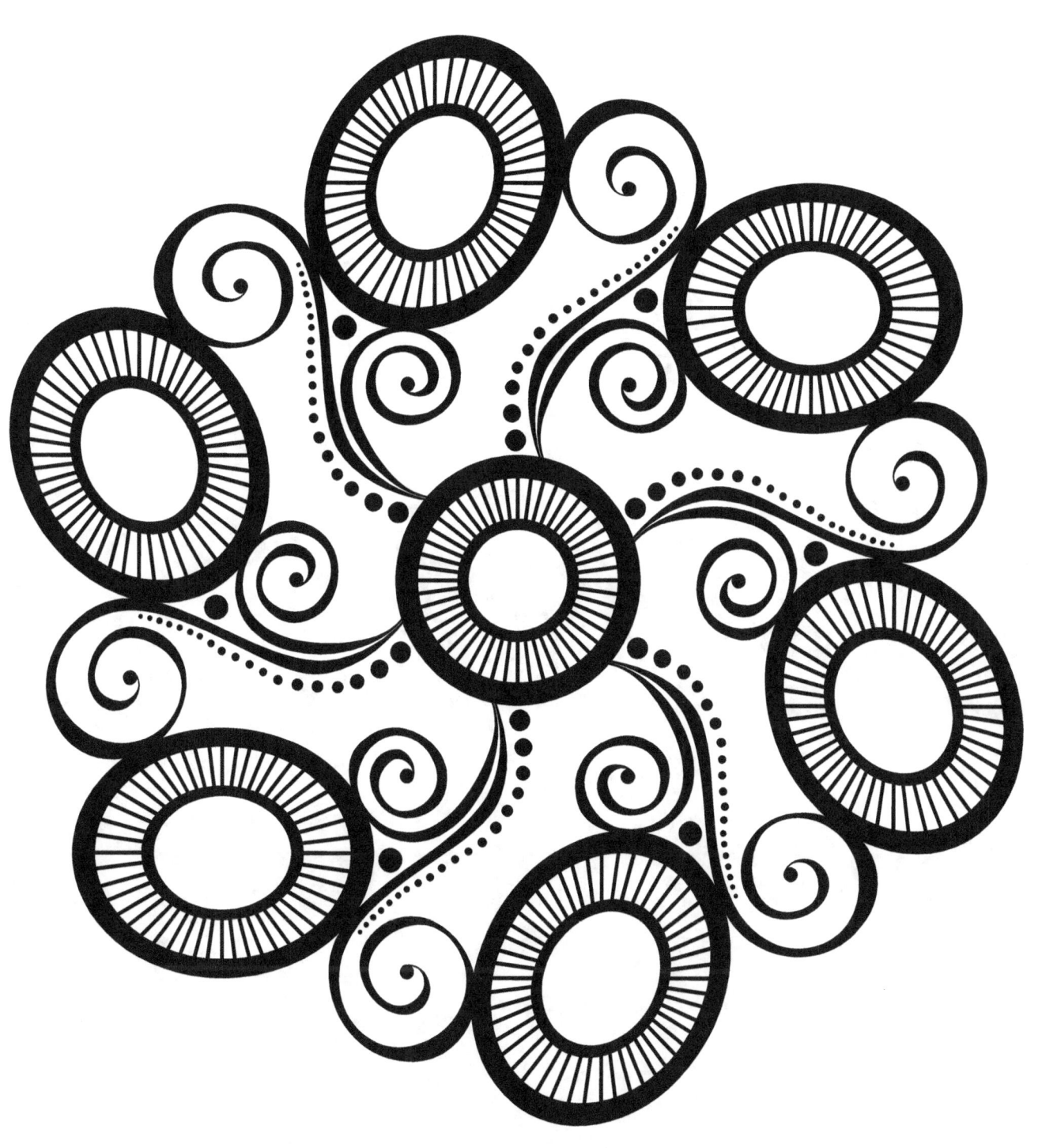

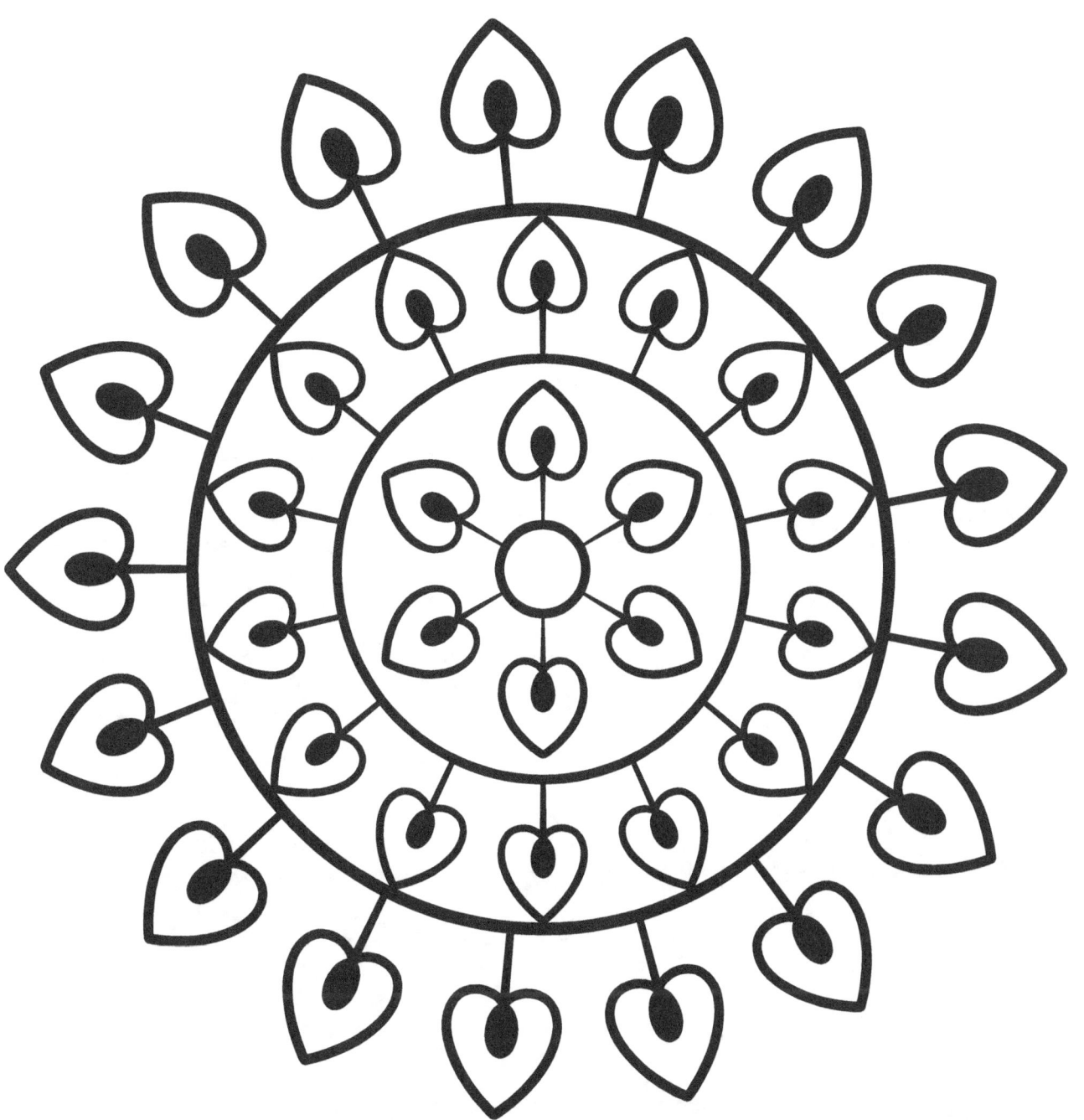

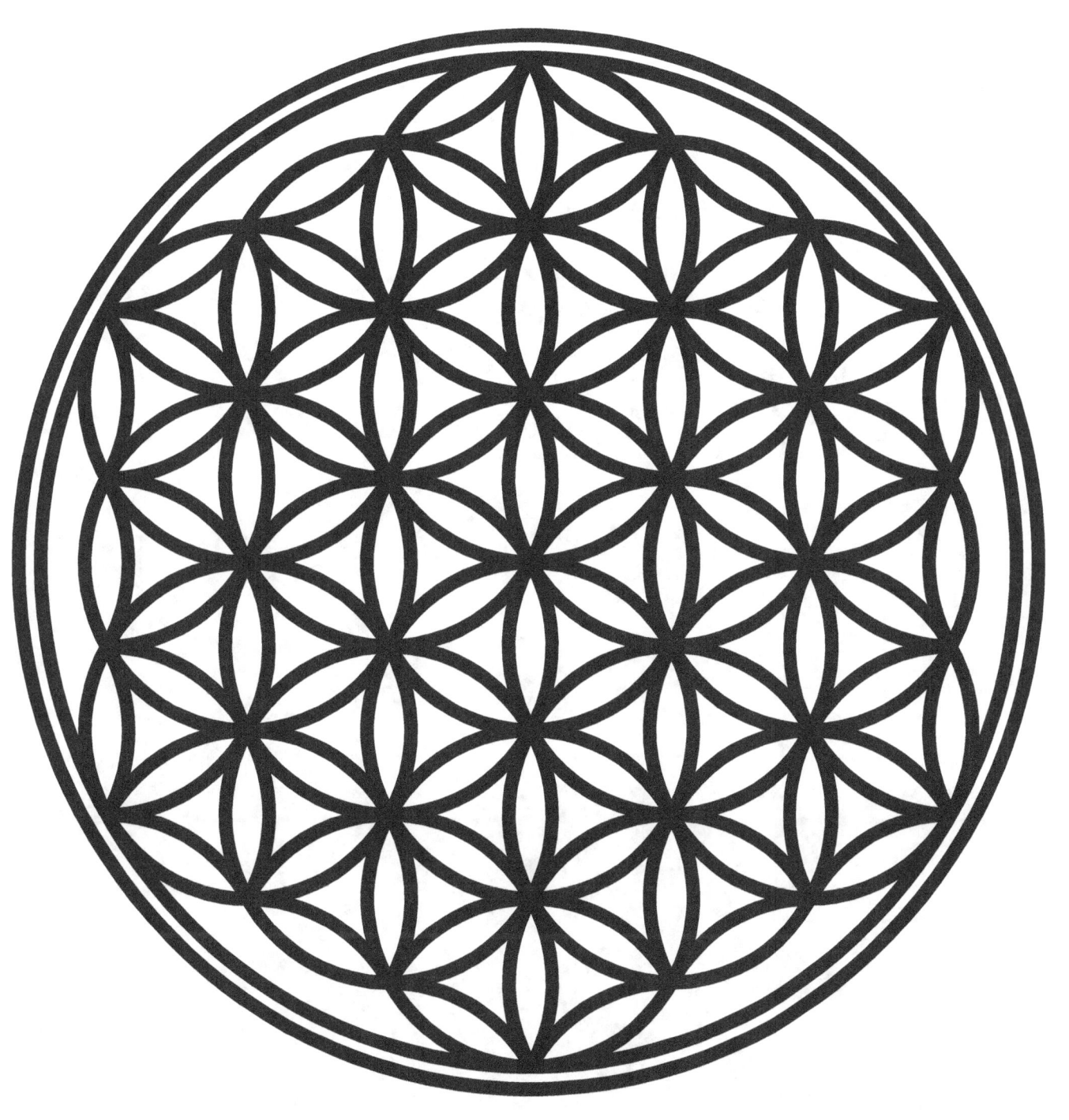

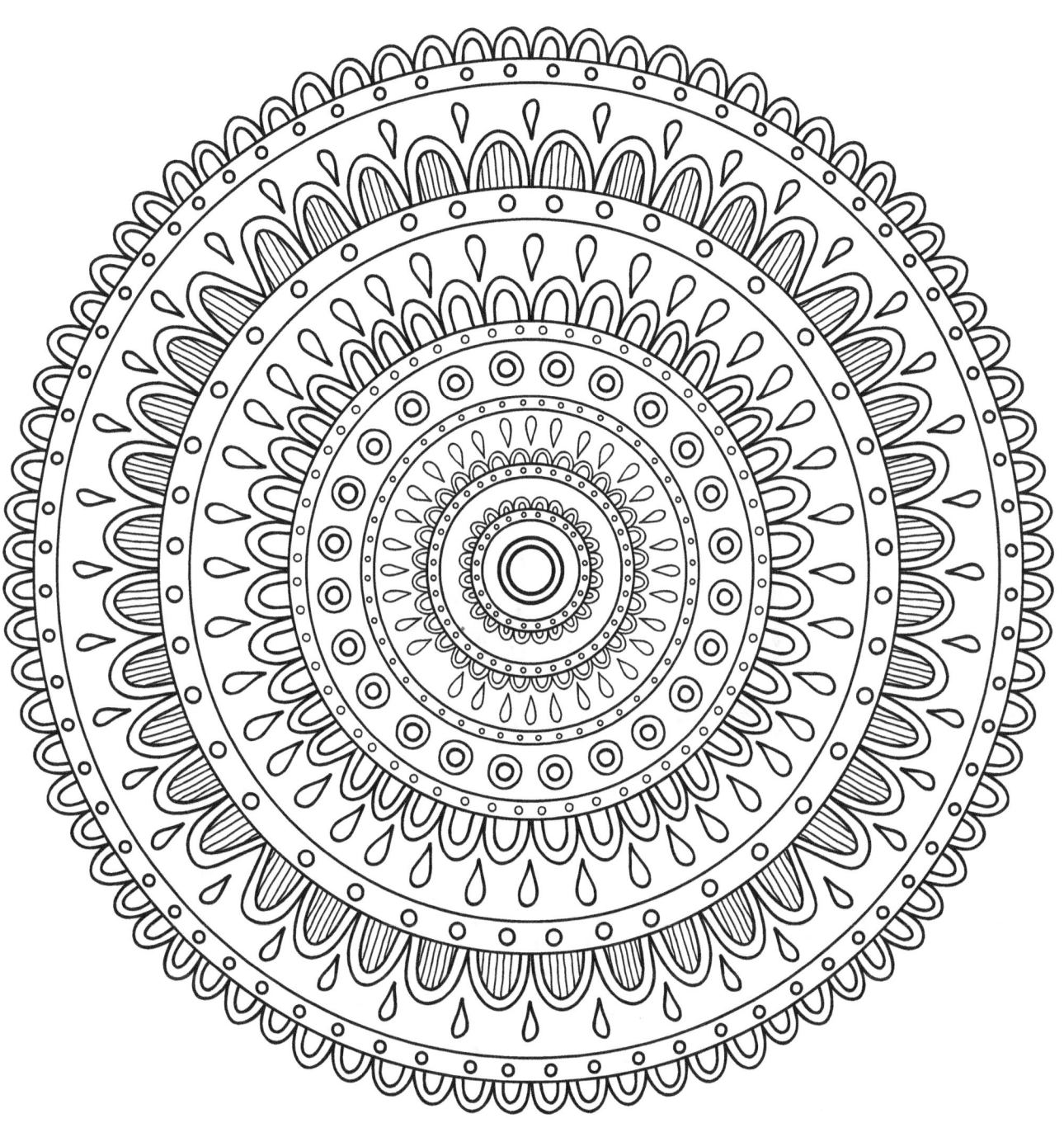

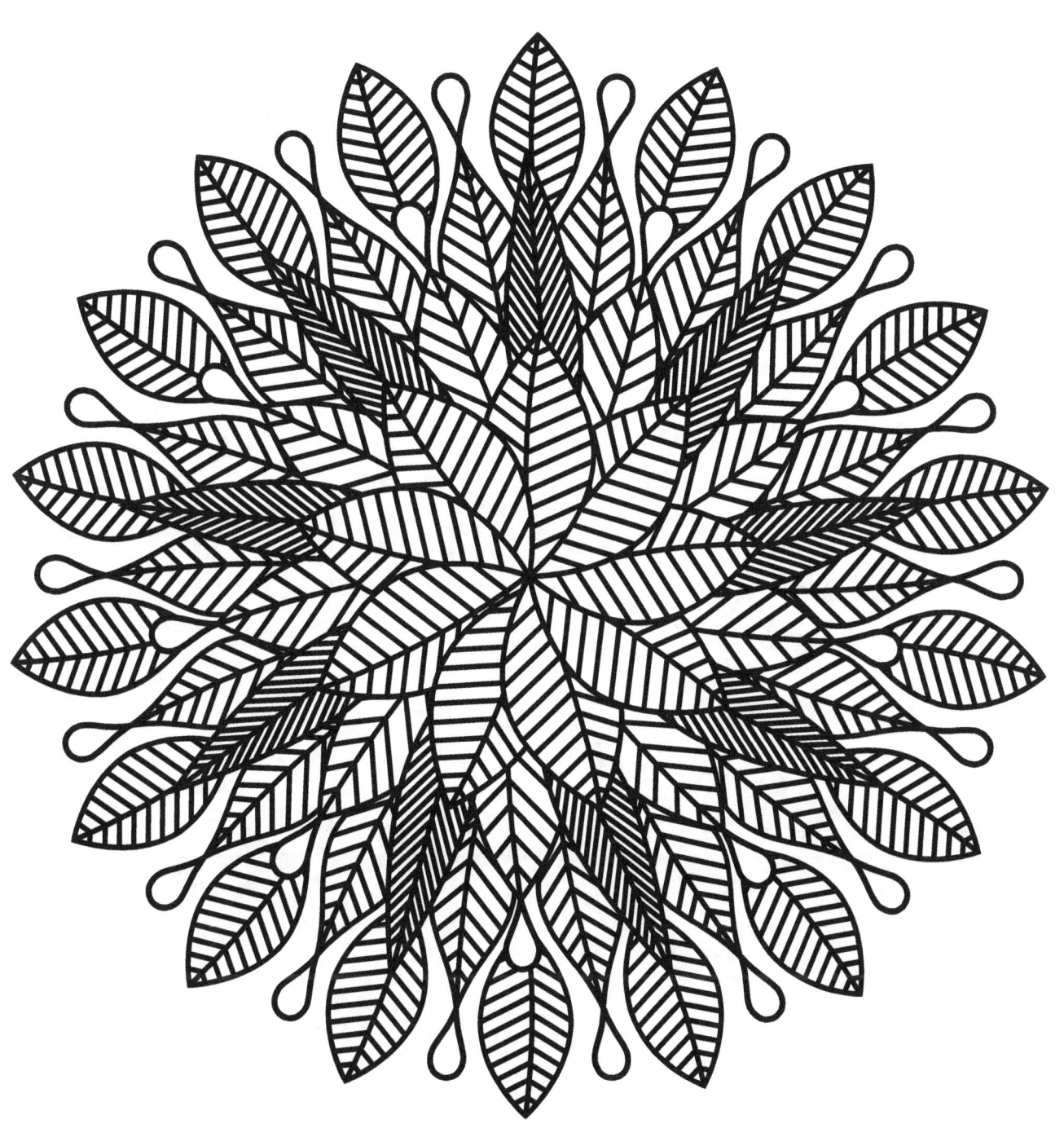

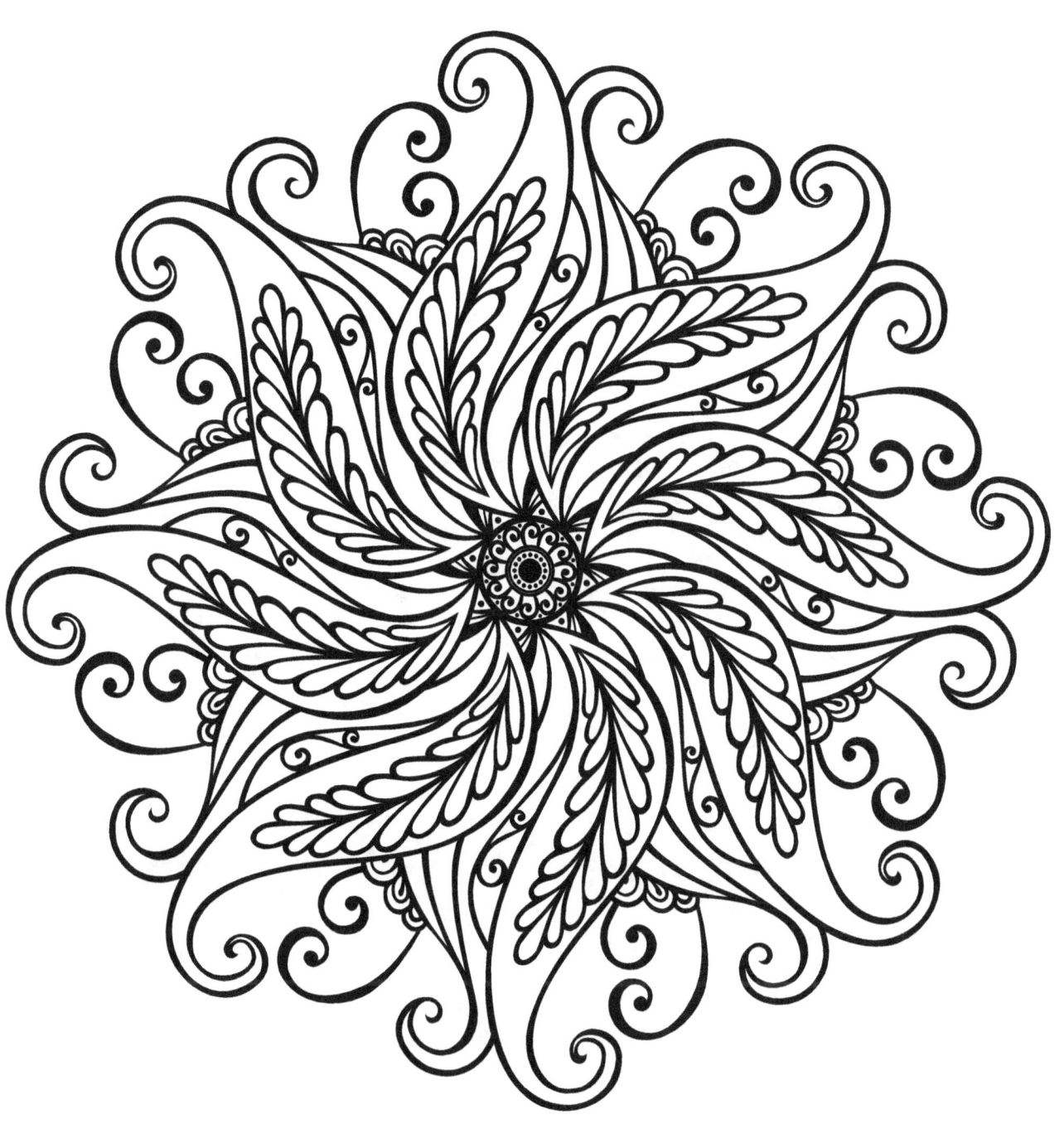

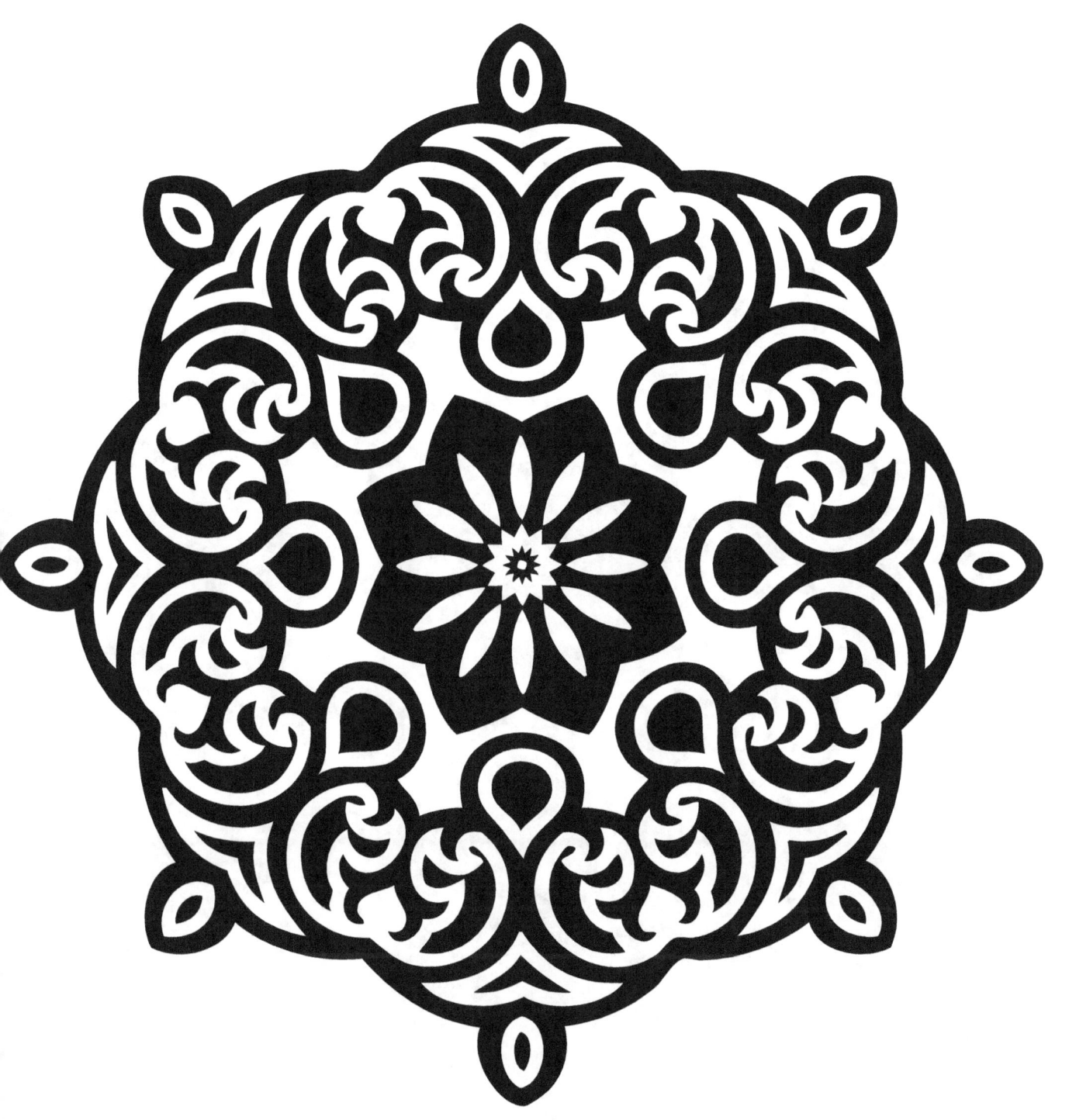

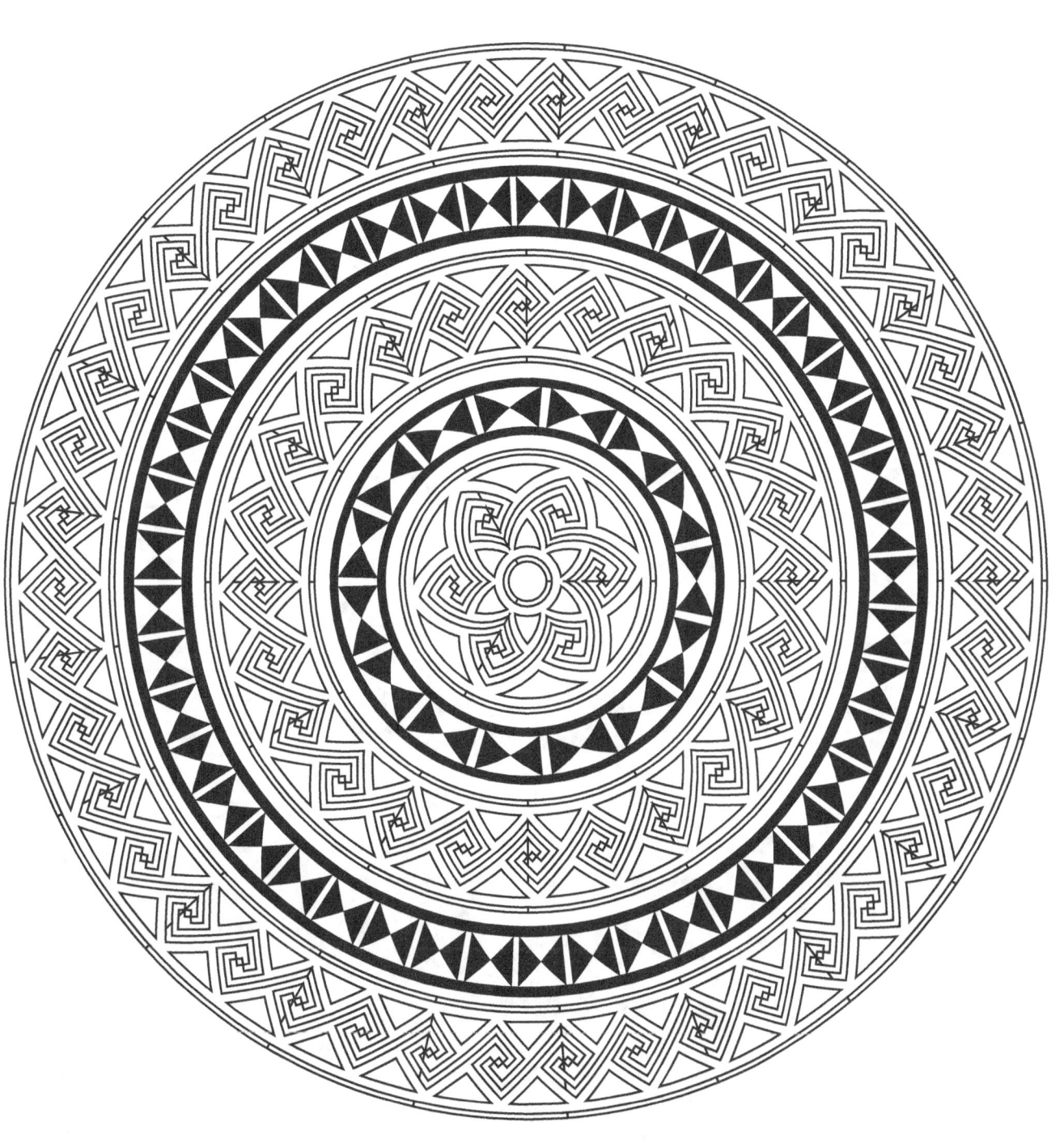

# Sample Images From
# Mandala Happiness 2
## Mandala Coloring Book

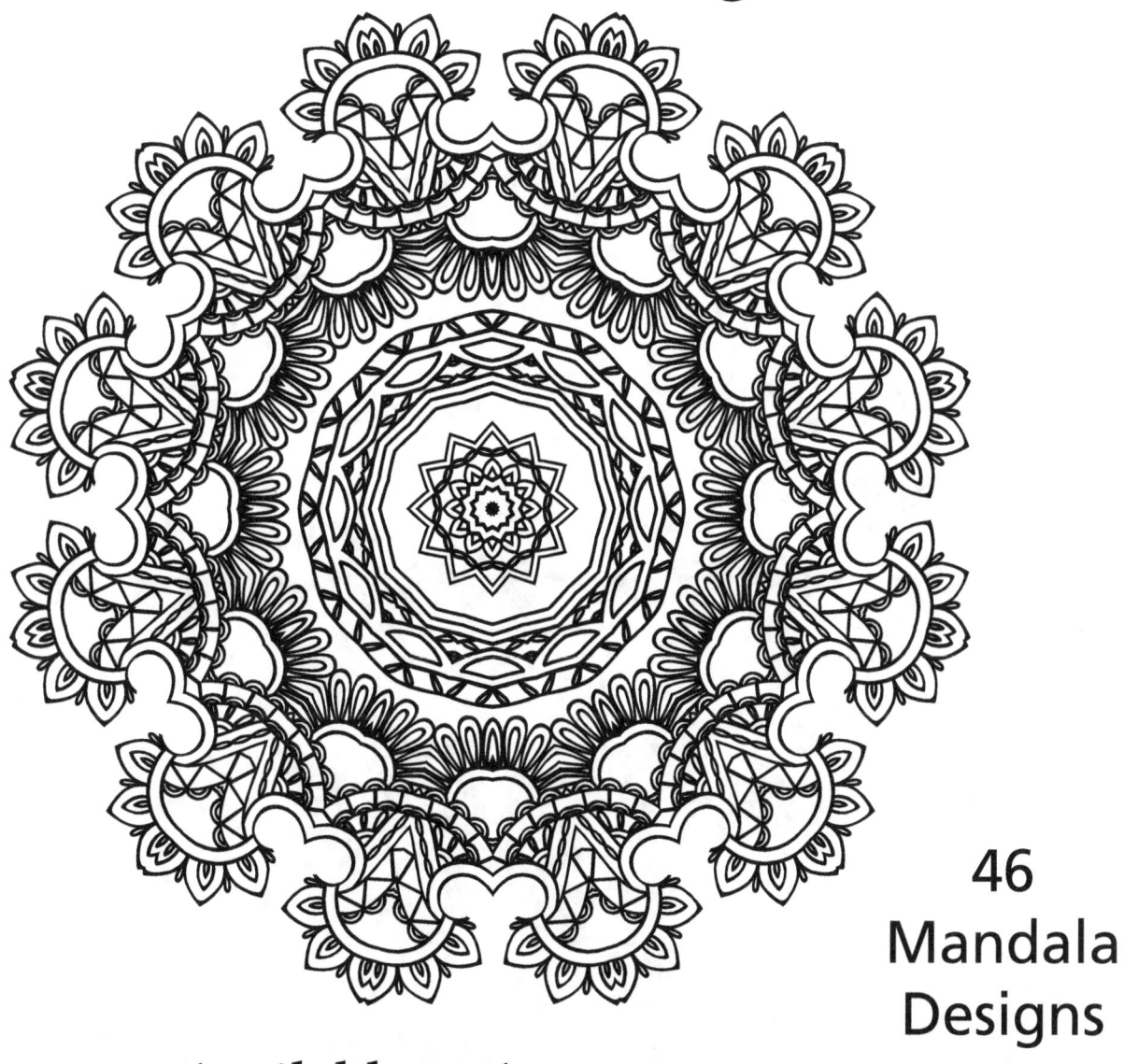

46
Mandala
Designs

## Available at Amazon.com

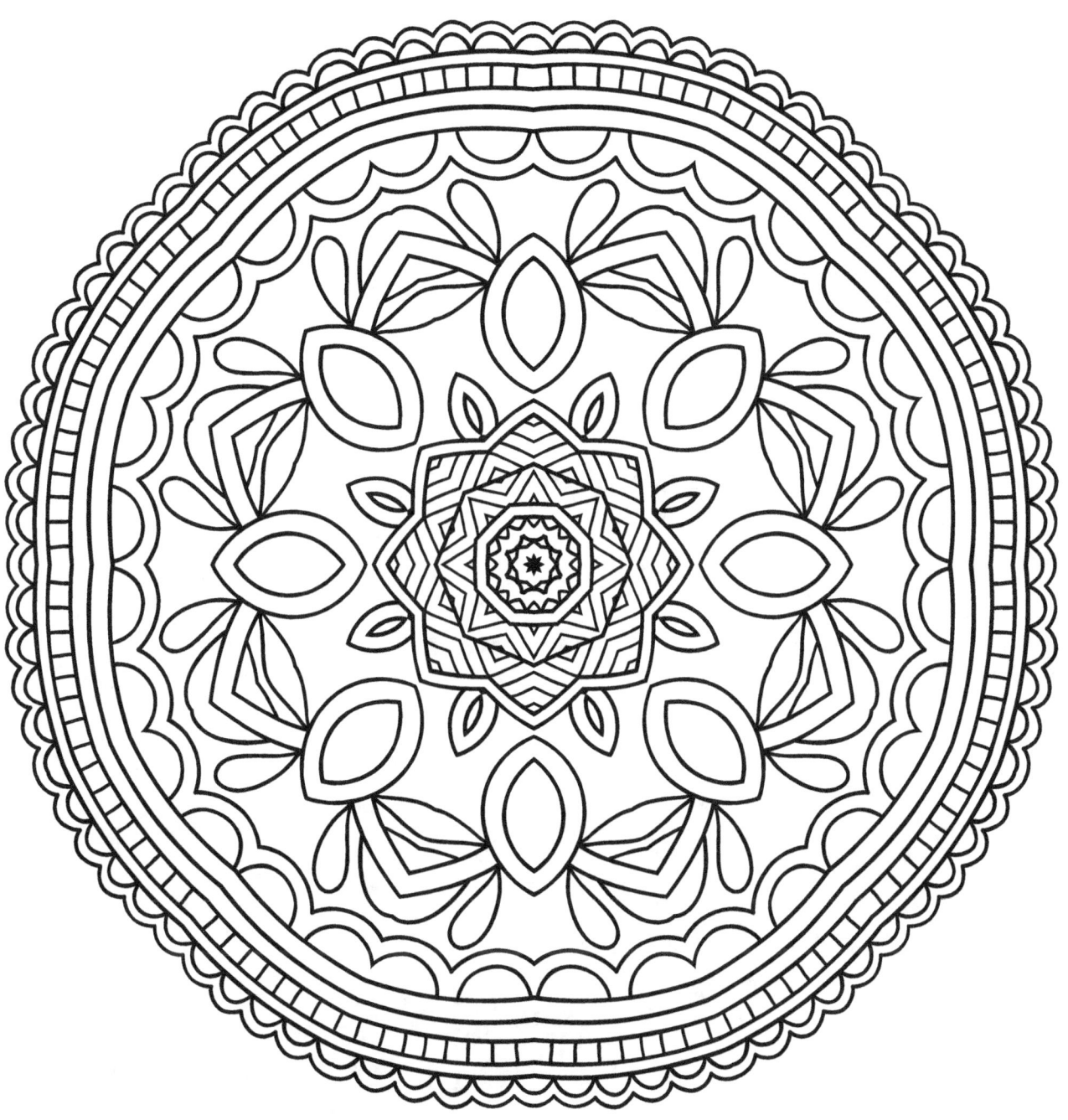

Sample Image From Mandala Happiness 2

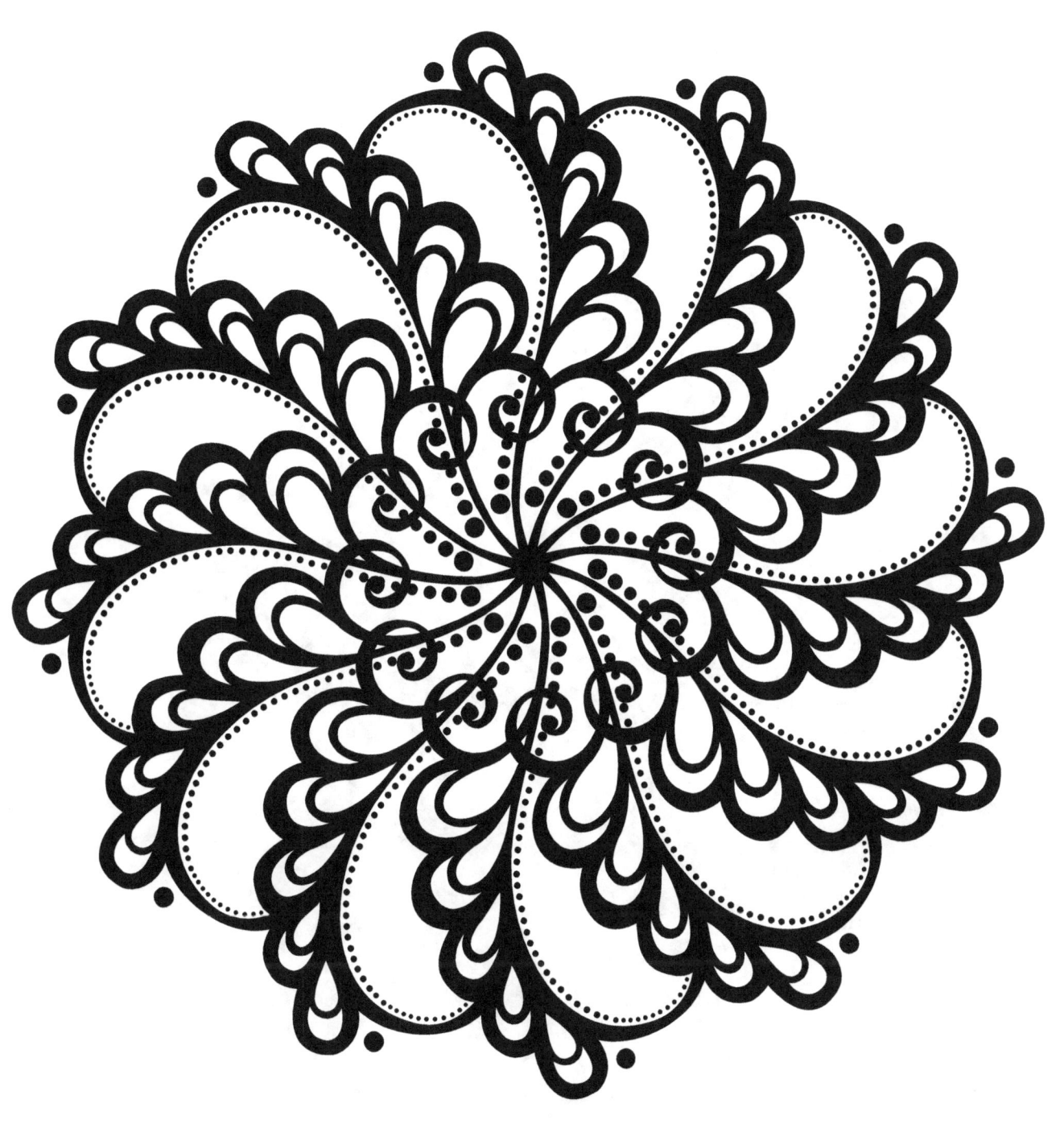

Sample Image From Mandala Happiness 2

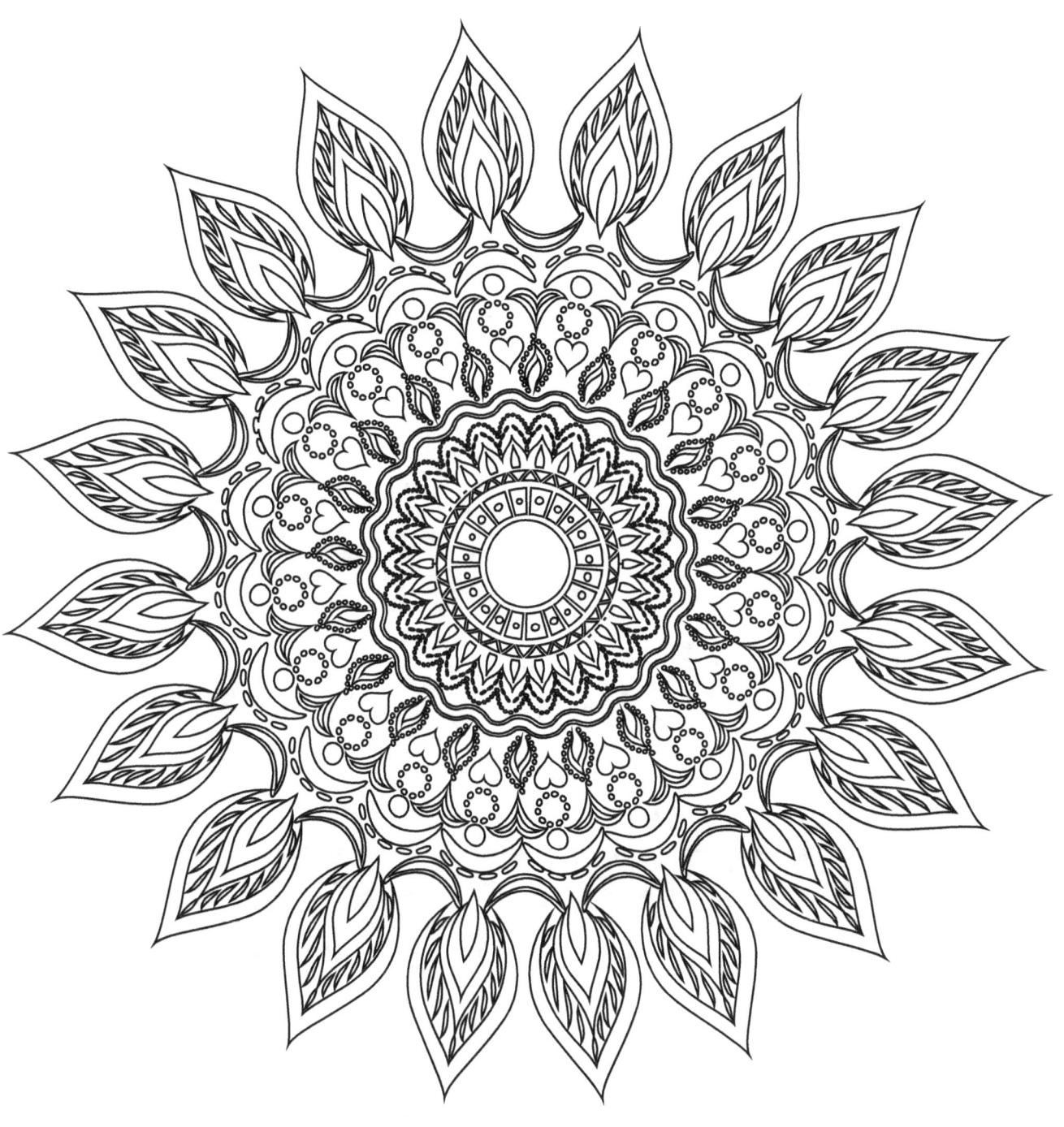

Sample Image From Mandala Happiness 2

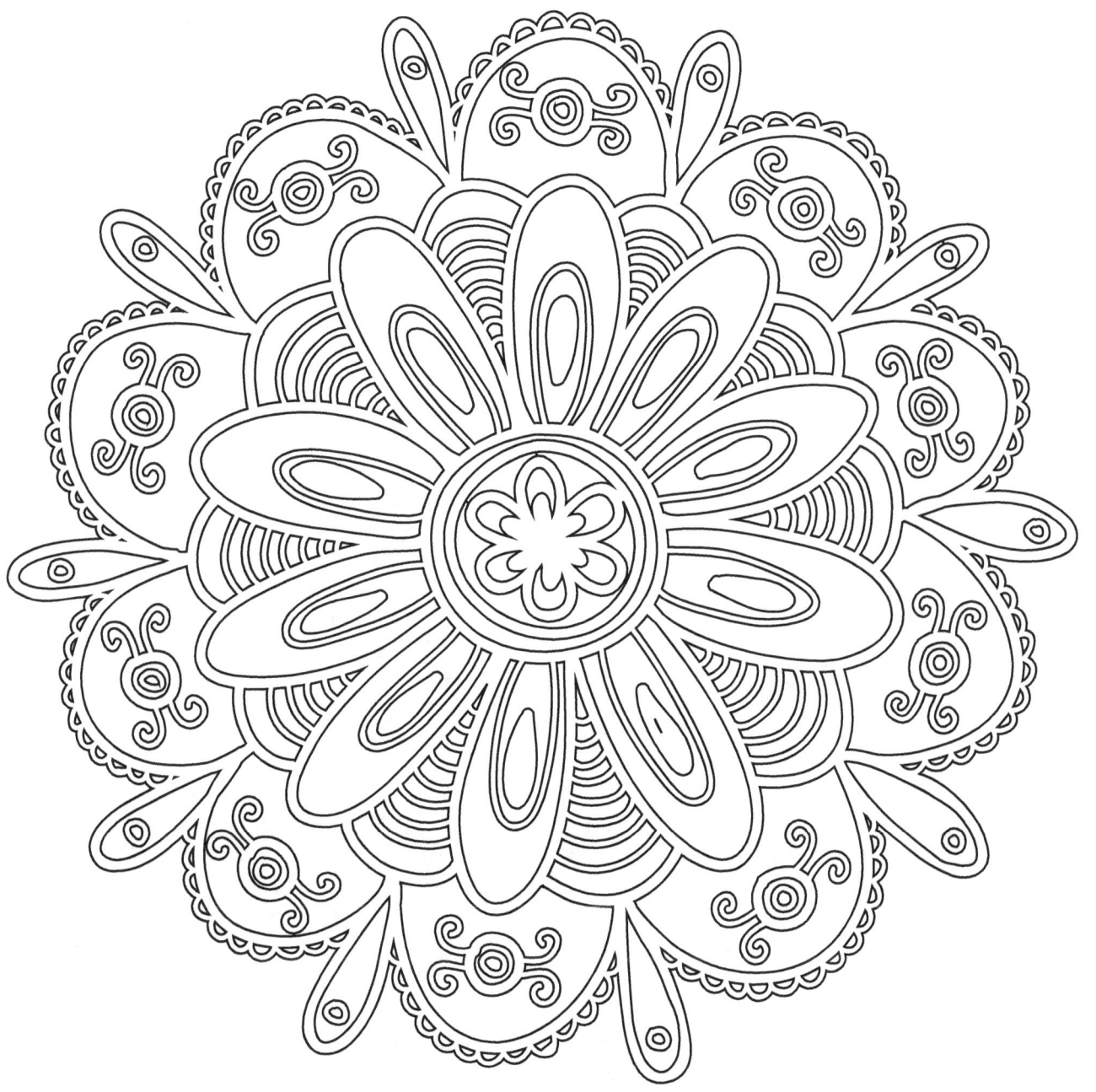

Sample Image From Mandala Happiness 2

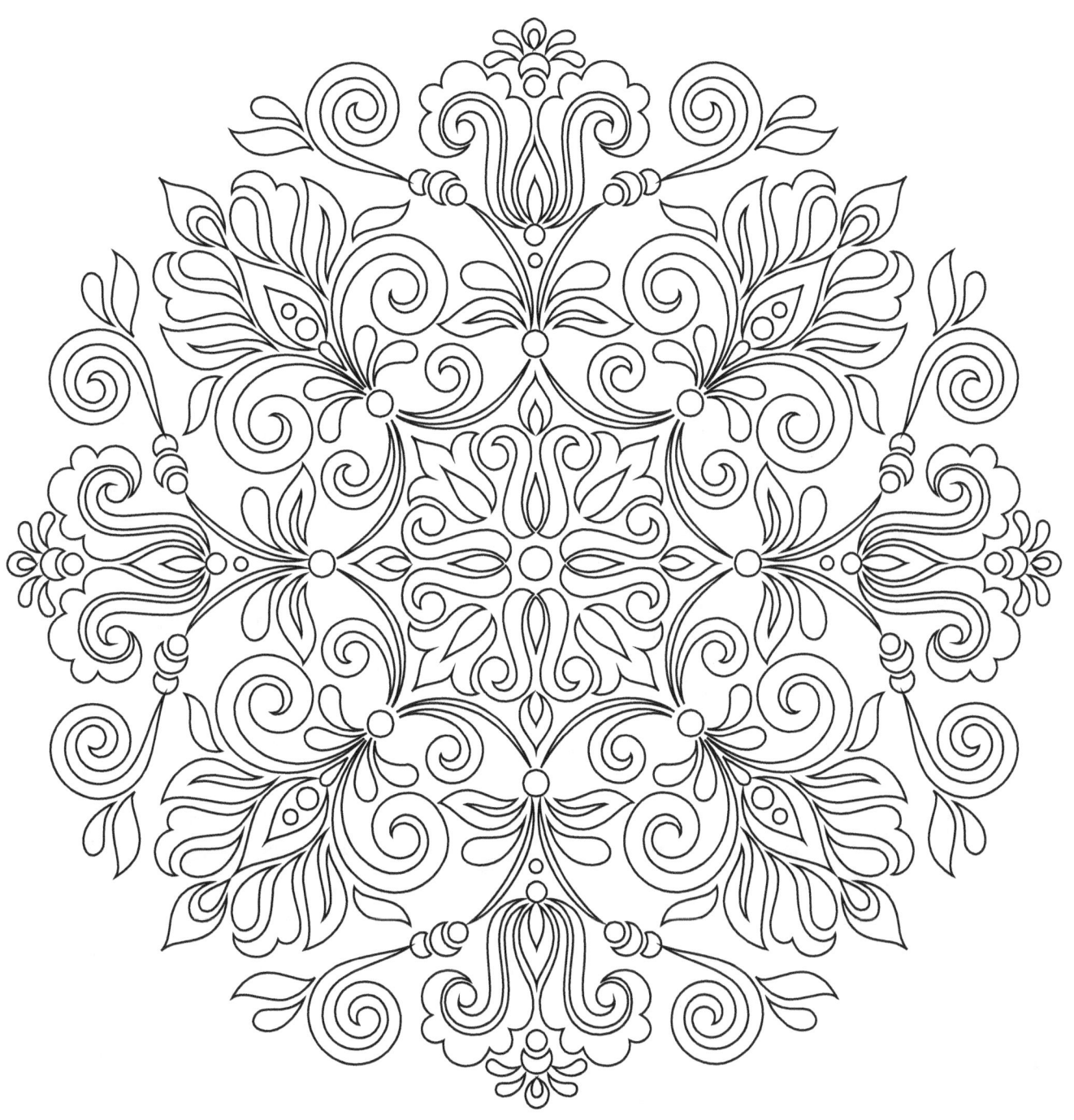

Sample Image From Mandala Happiness 2

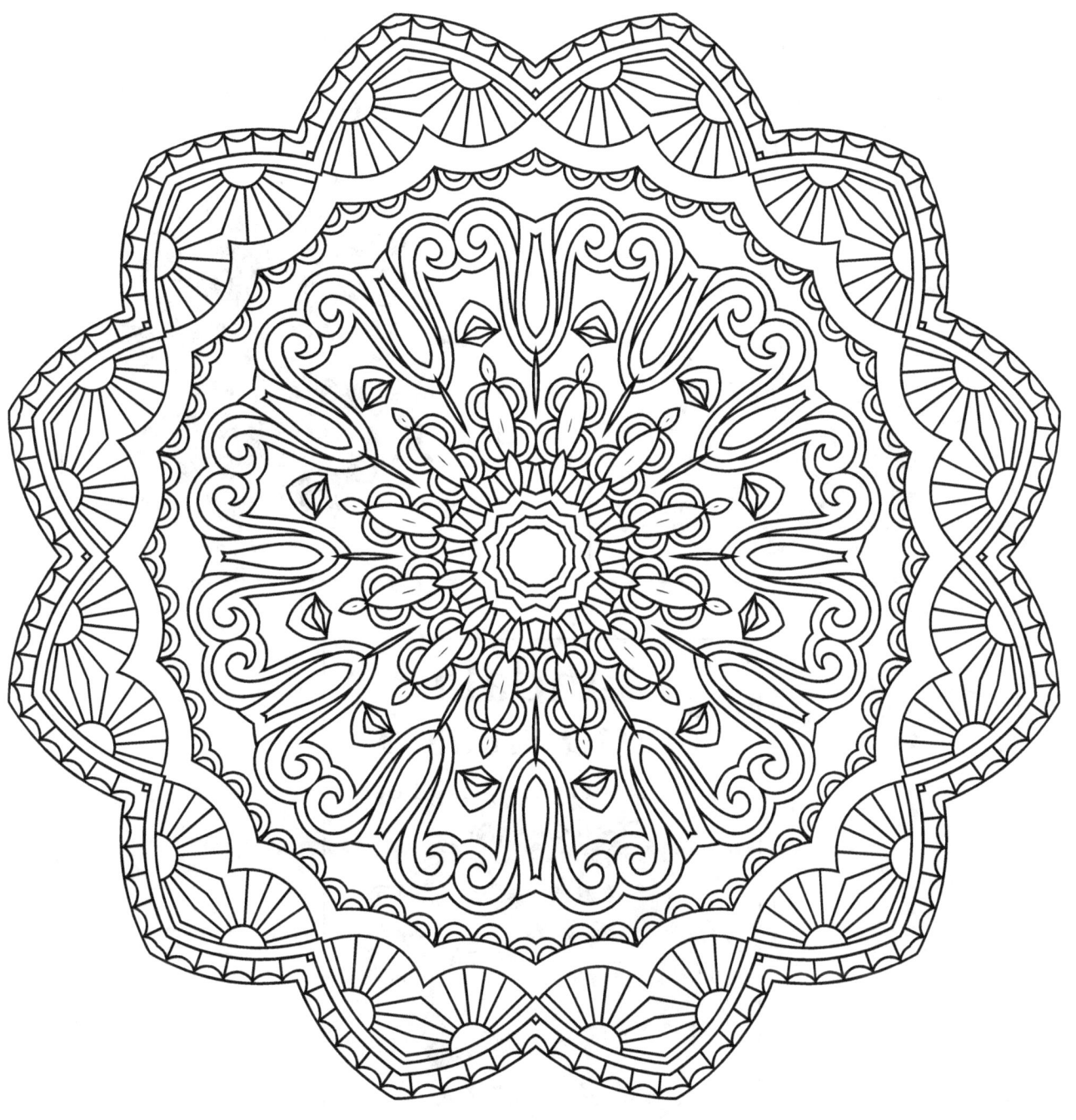

Sample Image From Mandala Happiness 2

# Mandala Happiness

Mandala Happiness Books Are Available at Amazon.com

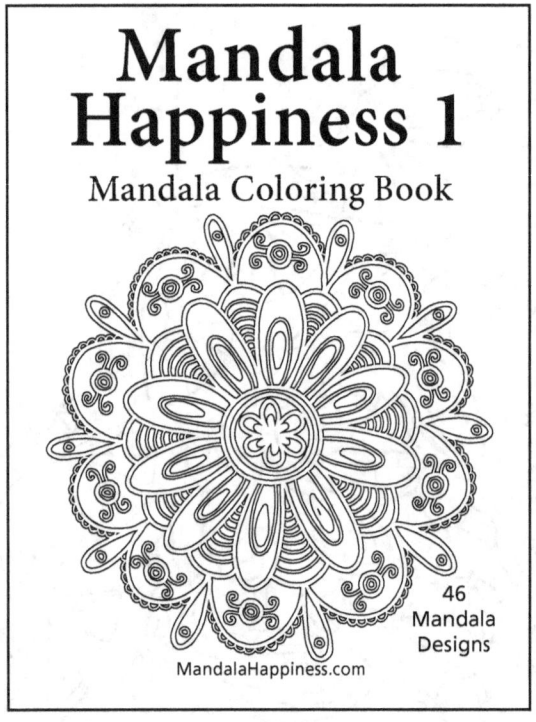

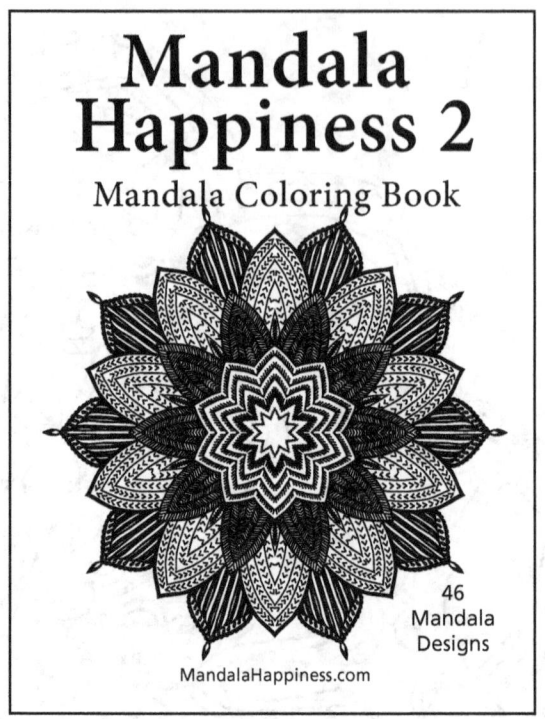

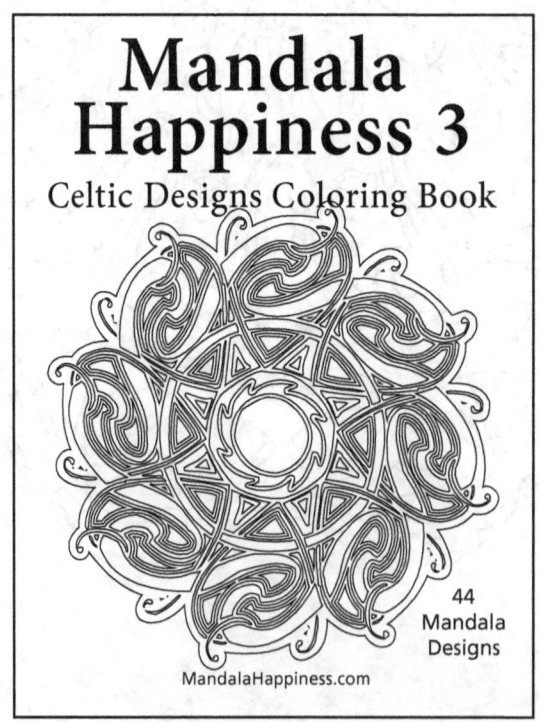

See all our books at MandalaHappiness.com

www.ingramcontent.com/pod-product-compliance
Lightning Source LLC
Chambersburg PA
CBHW080828180526
45168CB00006B/2605